Through the Eyes of the Child:
Survival of the Holocaust

Visit www.booksurge.com to order additional copies.

JACK
VEFFER

THROUGH THE EYES OF THE CHILD: SURVIVAL OF THE HOLOCAUST

2007

Through the Eyes of the Child: Survival of the Holocaust

FOREWORD BY DR. LEAH BRADSHAW
Associate Professor for Political Science at Brock University

I have spent much of my life as a scholar and teacher trying to understand the evils that human beings bring upon themselves and the world. The Holocaust is something that I did not experience, and I am neither a European nor a Jew. As a university student, I nonetheless became preoccupied with the fate of the Jews in the 20th century through my encounter with the books written by Hannah Arendt, the great Jewish philosopher and chronicler of totalitarianism. Hannah Arendt's family, like Jack Veffer's family, were assimilated European Jews, highly cultured, secular and enlightened. They saw themselves as full participants in the modern ethos of humanitarian equality. They did not expect to be secluded, interned and ultimately murdered by their fellow citizens. Traditional theories of enmity among human beings point to differences of class, colour, ethnic identity and habituation. The European Jews do not fit into any of these theories. Perhaps this is why the Holocaust stands out as the most horrific and unfathomable of genocides. One could not tell the difference between a Jew and a Gentile, unless one branded the Jews labeled them as a people apart. Even when the Nazis did this, the Jews of Europe for a long time did not really believe in the turn of their fellow citizens against them. It seemed too surreal to be true. In **The Origins of Totalitarianism** (N.Y. Harcourt Brace and Co, 1955), Hannah Arendt goes to great length to try to understand the *inexplicable*. "What common sense and 'normal' people refuse to believe is that everything is possible. We attempt to understand elements in present or recollected experience that simply surpass our powers of understanding."(p. 441)

Arendt's view, infamously depicted in her account of Adolph Eichmann's trial (**Eichmann in Jerusalem: A Report on the Banality of Evil**, N.Y., Viking Press, 1963) was that the worst things of which human beings are capable can not be theoretically understood, because evil is really a blackness, a void. It has no substantive content. It cannot be thought about, or written about. It can only be evoked as an absence of the real and the good. In her protracted attempts to understand the Holocaust, Arendt came to the conclusion that evil is never "radical, that it is only extreme, and that it possesses neither depth nor any demonic dimension. It can overgrow and lay waste the whole world precisely because it spreads like a fungus on the surface. It is 'thought defying', because thought tries to reach to some depth, to go to the roots, and the moment it concerns itself with evil, it is frustrated because there is nothing. That is its banality. Only the good has depth and can be radical." (Hannah Arendt, Letter to Gershom Scholem, New York City, July 24, 1963, reprinted in Ron Feldman, ed, The **Jew as Pariah**, N.Y., Grove Press, 1978, p. 251).

It seems to me that what Jack Veffer's book does for us is to fill in, as far as that is possible, the "recollected experience" that surpasses understanding. We get a remarkable unedited look at the confusion of the world from the standpoint of a child born and raised in the midst of Europe's darkest time. The mood of this book is stark and terse, although the text is rich in particular details of food, landscape, the emotional states of the people that surrounded Jack. Jack understands nothing, as a child, of the winds of politics, race and religion, but he experiences all these things and he learns to survive. The evil of the Holocaust is present on every page in the sorrows and the losses of this child, and what stands out for us is a vital example of Hannah Arendt's thoughts on evil: Jack hangs on to, and longs for, what is good. His book opens with the trust and the warmth of his mother's embrace. We experience through young Jack's senses not the presence of evil, but the absence of good.

What Jack learns is to retreat as far as possible into himself, from a world that is unstable and threatening. His parents have been taken away on a train to a death camp, he and his brother have been shunted from one unwilling guardian to another, and there have been periods of severe hunger, illness and deprivation. On his eighth birthday, he writes: "I realize, sadly, that I do not belong here, unfortunately I have nowhere else to go. So I try to make the best of it by being as unobtrusive as possible. I love to read. I have only one book that the teacher gave me at school. Reading it over and over, I enjoy it so very much. Speaking is not my strong suit because I don't really want to be noticed. I become an expert at not being seen. I can be in a room full of people and nobody will see me. It is as if I can make myself invisible. I practice doing that." (p. 122)

Jack's retreat into himself is noble, and saves him from despair, but it is a hard road. His childhood is filled with lies, misrepresentations, and false identity. Jack's writing of this book at the other end of his life, living in Canada, with a family of his own, under a democratic state, and his sharing of these experiences with others, one may regard as a cathartic and culminating stage in his life. The solitary person, Hannah Arendt writes, is alone and can be "together with himself" since men have the capacity of "talking with themselves". This capacity for solitude, Arendt was sure, is what saves human beings in traumatic situations from going mad. Nonetheless, solitude is not the most desirable state for a human being, and it takes courage to leave the refuge of solitude and confront the world again. The real meaning of courage, again from Hannah Arendt, is "present in a willingness to act and speak at all, to insert oneself into the world and begin a story of one's own… courage and boldness are already present in leaving one's private hiding place and showing who one is, in disclosing and exposing oneself." (**The Human Condition,** Chicago, University of Chicago Press, 1958, p. 186)

I like to think of this book as the act that makes Jack 'whole'. By evoking for us in his lucid and humble way the memories of a child who survived the Holocaust, Jack finds companionship in words. We do see him.

Dr. Leah Bradshaw
St. Catharines, Ontario
January 17, 2006

INTRODUCTION

Jackboots pounding on thundering pavement
Ancient Amsterdam cowering in self-conscious agony.
Marianne and Joseph, adoringly, gaze upon their newborn
I stare, with yet unseeing eyes, at their worried faces.
Hitler declares war on the world and
Vows to exterminate the Jews.
Humanity's silence is deafening
It is October 12, 1940.

***

All sorrows can be borne if you can put them into a story or tell a story about them".

Arendt Hannah; *(The Human Condition, first published in 1958.)*

***

This story is the story of murder, mass murder, on a scale hitherto unknown, premeditated and committed in cold blood. The murderers were German and the murdered, the Jews of Holland. The Jews were, in a process of disenfranchisement and isolation, robbed of everything, transported and in a systematic-scientific, technically-efficient manner, murdered.

They were city folk and farmers, orthodox, agnostic and atheist, healthy and sick, old and young, families and individuals, Dutch and Aliens: men, women and children.

Without hurry, well thought out, registered and regimented.

The murderers were often not brutes nor illiterates, but

academics and intellectuals with an abiding love for literature, sculpture and music: many were caring fathers and mothers and during the holiday season celebrated Christmas and thereafter resumed their labour: the murder of countless men, women and children, defenseless people, fellow human beings.

This is but one story, as seen through the eyes of one child, there are millions more.

CHAPTER 1
The War

***

During the night of May 9, 1940 the German army traversed the border into Holland. This fact rang in a new era for the Dutch population, and signified a major shift in the history of Dutch Jews. An ominous shift, whose outcome most Jews could scarcely fathom.

Neither fight nor flights were options contemplated. After all, it was thought; were not the Jews of Holland full and equal partners in the fabric of everyday life?

Jews could proudly point to the many accomplishments in the arts, medicine and the sciences by such well known Jewish scholars as Baruch Spinoza, Martin Buber, Herman Cohen, Moses Mendelssohn, Sigmund Freud, Albert Einstein, and world renowned artists, Jan Peerce, Robert Merrill, Jascha Heifetz, Mischa Elman, Isaac Stern and Arthur Rubenstein, to name but a few. Their accomplishments accruing to the good of all mankind. The Jews of Holland considered themselves Dutch, first and foremost. When a neighbour asked my father: "And you, what will you do?" "Nothing," he answered in a loud voice "Why should we?" When the German troops passed by in perfect goose-step he murmured: "See, they don't bother with us."

***

As I drink my fill from mother's swollen breast, Maurice is watching this wondrous sight.

"Mommy, can I have some too?" he asks.

"No son, Jackie is only one and you're five years old now. You have to drink from a cup" She replies with a smile.

Looking down at him with half opened eyes, I am content.

Daddy can no longer work at the diamond factory. The factory is closed because nobody wants to buy diamonds.

***

Paper currency is quickly losing its value; there are those that look upon owning diamonds as a hedge against the devaluation of the currency.

'The business' is the name that Jewish diamond workers call their work.

Many Jews are employed in the Amsterdam diamond industry. Amsterdam was the most important center for finished diamonds in the world; before the Second World War.

No Guild exists for this industry so that Jewish newcomers from other countries such as Spain, Germany and Portugal could, since the seventeenth century, engage in this trade.

The Sephardim Jews have always had international relations in areas where diamonds are traditionally being mined, mainly South Africa, and so they became the most important diamond traders in Amsterdam.

The actual making of a diamond, from rough into a finished polished diamond, is also mostly in Jewish hands. Early on, the cutting of a diamond occurred at home, in attics. The cutting machines were operated by the cutters feet to make the cutting wheel spin. In later years, as production increased, factories were set up and the cutting wheels were steam driven.

Most diamonds came from South Africa and in the period before the war the diamond industry in Amsterdam was one of the most important centers in the world.

***

Daddy told Mommy that he sold some of his diamonds for money. Now he can buy food for us.

Daddy complains to Mommy: "Seiss-Inquart, the German Reichskommissar, has stolen our money out of the bank account. Thank goodness, I hid some of the money in the house."

He takes Mommy to the cupboard in the kitchen and he takes down a shoebox. When he opens the box I see lots of money. Some of it falls on the floor. I help to pick it up and put it back in the shoebox.

***

Food is scarce. To procure food, people travel great distances, usually at night, to the farms outside Amsterdam to get a few potatoes and vegetables. Meat and eggs can be obtained at exorbitant prices. Securing food for the family is a full time job.

"No Jewish community in Western Europe suffered more during the Holocaust than the Jews of Holland. Out of a prewar population of 140,000 (including 15,000 refugees from Nazi Austria and Germany), barely 30,000 Dutch Jews survived the four years of Nazi terror. A lucky handful escaped the death camps by fleeing before the invasion. But most of those who survived the war in Holland did so by hiding with the help of a network of brave countrymen who risked their own lives for the sake of others— usually total strangers."

(Richard Chesnoff, *Pack of Thieves*)

***

Outside the house I can hear the wind howl. I shiver. It is very cold in the house. Daddy can get a few pieces of coal from time to time so the kitchen stove is only used for cooking. We all circle around to get warm for a while. Daddy has long ago burnt the little bit of wood he found from things we don't need around the house and pieces he found outside. Mommy dresses me in warm clothes to try to keep me cozy.

There is no electricity. We have to use candles for light.

We manage to get through the winter of 1942.

"Life is very hard." Daddy complains. "But, see, I told you that the Germans would leave us alone. They know we are Dutch citizens, and that counts for something. We pose no threat to them." He adds with hope in his voice.

Mommy and Daddy don't go outside much. When they do, they have to wear a big yellow Star of David on their coat so that every one knows that they are Jews.

They talk softly to each other. They think I can't hear what they're saying. Daddy says he is not so sure now that we won't get picked up in one of the many raids.

***

"When Hitler came to power in 1933, Dutch Jews began to feel the consequences at once. Caring for and housing refugees from Germany and Austria became a major concern: an estimated 34,000 of them arrived in Holland between 1933 and 1940. The government left the organization and financing of refugee relief to the Jewish community but required that it put up a guarantee of one million guilders. A tough policy was introduced to stem the growing tide of refugees after the anti-Jewish violence of Kristallnacht (November 8-9, 1938): entire groups were sent back across the German border. The government forced the Jewish community to intern refugees in Westerbork—later used by the Nazis as a transit camp for deportees to the death camps. Except among Socialists, the Jews, and especially German Jews, were increasingly viewed as a problem."

(Edward van Voolen, Curator of the Jewish Historical Museum, Amsterdam.)

Anton Mussert, who was appointed as the leader of the NSB, the Dutch fascist party, was a great admirer of the Italian fascist leader Benito Mussolini and copied many of his political ideas. He shared 'il Duce's' hatred towards democracy and egalitarianism.

Mussert claimed that Holland needed a powerful central government that could provide strong rightist leadership for the Dutch.

Mussert also borrowed many of his political ideas from Adolph Hitler.

The NSB, as was Hitler's Nazi party, was anti-Semitic and in order to ingratiate himself to the German occupiers, co-operated with them to denounce Jews from their hiding places.

Informants were paid seven guilders per Jew (approximately 2 dollars). Once the Jews were rounded up they were sent to the labour camp of Westerbork and from there, packed in cattle cars, to Bergen Belsen, Theresienstadt, Buchenwald, Mauthausen, Sobibor or Auschwitz.

Mussert overestimated his own role and thought that Hitler had the best interest of the Dutch people in mind. The Germans and the Gestapo did not care for his political ideas. Their co-operation was forged because he was the only one with whom co-operation was possible.

Anton Adriaan Mussert, the symbol of treason, was convicted of collaboration with the enemy and shot on May 7, 1946.

"The heroism of Holland's savers is legendary: the anonymous volunteers who waited outside the internment center at Amsterdam's Hollandsche Schouwburg theater to catch children literally tossed over the wall in a frantic last-minute attempt to save them from deportation; the underground railroad of workers, housewives, students, and clergy who passed fugitive Jews from one to the other, then sheltered them in attics, in basements or in the case of the smallest children, raised them as their own; the brave souls like the gentle Miep Gies who at enormous risk to herself and her own kin helped hide three Jewish families, among them a young girl named Anne Frank.

But Holland's Anne Franks were few in number, and even the twelve-year-old diarist whose notebooks came to symbolize the Holocaust ultimately was betrayed by a Dutchman.

For every Dutch Jew saved, ten others were shipped to their deaths for lack of neighbours willing to help within hours of their arrest on August 4, 1944; the hiding place of Anne Frank and her family was ransacked and looted. Some say by her Dutch neighbours, others by the Dutch-owned, Nazi-hired Puls moving company."

(Richard Chesnoff's, Pack of Thieves pgs.)

"This country took care of very few Anne Franks," says Dutch economist Victor Halberstadt, himself a hidden child during three years of the war. "The government did not protect us during the war. And when those of us who survived came back, the government was not particularly interested in us."

Says Ed Van Voolen: "The Nazi invasion, took the Dutch by surprise. For the Dutch Jews, a tolerated and never-persecuted minority, it comes as a crushing blow. The country was placed under a civil administration led by virulent anti-Semites like Arthur Seiss-Inquart (1892-1946) and Hans Rauter (1895-1949), who quickly introduced anti-Jewish legislation. On October 18, 1940, civil servants and students were required to prove they were not of Jewish descent.

October 22, 1940, Jewish business owners must register their businesses.

November 4, 1940, all Jews were dismissed from the civil service.

The High Court, the country's supreme judicial body, submitted and approved the removal of its own president, Lodewijk Ernst Visser, a Jew.

Protest amounted to a handful of Christian leaders and students.

January 10, 1941, the Nuremberg race law of 1935, defining anyone with three Jewish grandparents as a Jew, was implemented in Holland.

An ensuing skirmish at the start of February 1941, protesting the law, caused the Germans to seal off the old Jewish quarter in Amsterdam.

Emulating existing Nazi policy in Eastern Europe, a Jewish Council, composed of the leaders of prewar Amsterdam Jewish leaders, was set up on February 13, 1941.

February 22-23, 1941, a round-up of 425 young Jews on Jonas Daniël Meijer Square, and forced onto a transport train to Buchenwald and Mauthausen, where they were soon murdered.

In protest the underground Communist party in Amsterdam provoked a strike. Although the strike was broken in three days, the event is now recognized as a true popular protest against the injustice being done to the Jews.

It was the start, however, of the large scale round-up of Jews everywhere in the Netherlands.

"On June 3, 1941, compulsory identity papers were issued: Jews' were stamped with a large J. On May 1, 1942, Jews were forced to wear a visible badge: a yellow star with the word Jood (Jew). A few months later, the Nazis turned the Hollandsche Schouwburg Theater on Plantage Middenlaan (where Jewish artists had been performing for exclusively Jewish audiences) into a collection point for Jews en route to the Westerbork transit camp. Between July 1, 1942 and September 13, 1944, a train of sealed cattle cars departed Westerbork every Tuesday morning, each taking an average of 1,000 to the death camps of Auschwitz and Sobibor or to Bergen Belsen and Theresienstadt.

"Of the nearly 80,000 Jews living in Amsterdam in 1941, barely 15,000 survived the war, in hiding or in concentration camps. Of the 140,000 Jews in the Netherlands at the start of the war, fewer than 30,000 (21%) were alive at its end."

(Edward van Voolen, Curator of the Jewish Historical Museum, Amsterdam.)

***

It is Passover and the family comes together at our house, 14 Christiaan de Wetstraat II, for Seder. Mommy and Daddy don't keep a kosher house, but they do follow the Jewish Holy day traditions. Some of my aunts, uncles, and their children are here. Many are missing because they have been taken by the bad German soldiers.

Mommy with eyes that are full of tears, says, in a voice filled with sadness, to no one in particular, but looking right at Maurice and me, as if she is trying to burn the names into our brains: "Missing are Opa and Oma, cousin Jacob Veffer and his wife Klaartje, Oma Bekkie Nebig, Aunt Rika Brilleslijper and her husband Jacob and their children, Jonas, Annie, Clara and Vrouwtje, Uncle Appie Veffer and his wife Hester and their children, Japie, Susanna and Jonas, Aunt Anna Veffer, Uncle Abraham Nebig, Aunt Esther Nebig, great Aunts Betje, Esther and Kaatje Nebig. Your Auntie Saar and Uncle Jonas and their children, are not here because they have recently gone into hiding."

**

An extra place is set at the table symbolizing the missing family members. The remainder of the family, hearts overflowing with sadness put on a cheerful face, hoping that the age-old Passover tradition of freedom for the Jews, and the promise of "Next year in Jerusalem" will come to pass.

Nobody talks much about the missing loved ones, for fear of inviting the worst kind of luck upon themselves. Those present are hoping fervently for better times to come. We share what little food we have. Everyone brings something.

**

Daddy says to Maurice: "as the youngest child here you may ask me the four age-old questions that have been asked since time immemorial." My brother happy that he was asked to do this by Daddy has been learning the questions with Mommy's help all afternoon. I heard them so much that I remember them all too.

"Daddy, why is this night different from all other nights?"

"On all other nights we eat all different kind of bread."

"Daddy, why do we eat only matzo on Passover?"

"Matzo reminds us that when the Jews left Egypt, they were in a hurry and they had no time to bake their bread. They took the unleavened dough with them on their journey and let it bake in the hot desert sun into hard unleavened bread called matzo."

"Daddy, why do we dip our food twice tonight?"

"We dip bitter herbs into Charoset, a mixture of nuts, cinnamon and apples, to remind us how hard the Jewish slaves had to work in Egypt. The chopped apples and nuts represent the clay that is used to make the bricks required to build Pharaoh's buildings. The parsley that we dip into salt water reminds us that spring is renewal time and new life is starting to grow. The salt water reminds us of the tears that the Jewish slaves shed."

"Daddy, on all other nights we eat sitting up, why do we recline on a pillow tonight?"

"We recline on a pillow to make us comfortable and to help us remember that we were slaves once, but that we are free now."

Some people are sobbing, while others push back the tears.

"God, if you love us so much and we are your favourite people, why do you make us suffer so?" Daddy muses.

The questions have a special meaning tonight, as if God might soon fulfill the Prophecies.

Daddy says a prayer for the family members that are missing.

***

The war has been raging, unabated, for about three years. Food and supplies are even scarcer now and the family comes together in secrecy, arriving a few at a time at intervals. Families support each other in the best way they can. Because of the night curfew imposed, the Seder is held during daylight hours as close to nighttime as possible.

***

Maurice counts the people that are in the house. At the number seventeen, he runs out of numbers.

"Mommy what number comes after seventeen?" he wants to know.

Mommy, thinking out loud replies:"Before the war we had fifty-three people in our family and now twenty-eight are missing. We are only twenty five left."

***

At war's end, only seventeen members of my immediate family remain.

***

The familiar smell of warm milk attracts me. I hunt for its source until I find it. I reach up and pull. The instant searing heat makes me drop the pot. It is too late. The boiling milk I pulled from the stove has burnt me on one side of my body. My shirt sticks to my flesh. Hands pull at it.

The screams confuse me. I hear myself scream.

The immense all-consuming burning pain has not yet registered in my brain.

Mommy and Daddy rush me to the hospital to take care of my badly burnt body.

Far off, I hear the doctors talk. "Third degree burns halfway up his left arms and on one third of his chest. Does not look good. Not much we can do. Only time will tell if he'll make it."

I drift off into a deep sleep.

A doctor with a mask on his face is pulling at my shirt, gently removing it from the burned parts. Someone pricks me with a needle. It hurts and then I feel no pain anymore.

Ice is being put on the burns and I feel very cold.

And so it goes. I wake up. The pain is awful. I scream and a nurse comes running. She gives me a needle and I start to feel sleepy. When I wake up someone is changing the bandages. I start to whimper and I get another needle. My arm and chest hurt so badly I scream and I scream, but the pain does not stop. They give me another needle. It does not help. Through closed eyes, I see Mommy sitting at the edge of the bed and she cries hysterically, while Daddy holds her. There is no end to the pain. The pain is so bad my soul screams.

**

There is a pall over the entire country. From time to time the resistance people carry out attacks on Germans. One such attack on SS Police Leader H. Rauter causes the summary execution of 230 Dutch men by the Gestapo.

"Under decree VO189/40, January of 1941 was the deadline for all Dutch Jews to register as full Jews, half Jews, or quarter Jews.

A total of 159,806 persons registered, according to Dutch-Jewish historian Jozeph Michman. Of these, 140,245 were "full Jews." The remaining 19,561 were halfbloeden, the children of mixed marriages.

To the Jews of Holland who shared the pedantic sense of orderliness of their Dutch-Christian neighbors, the Germans' rules were to be obeyed, no matter how odious.

"The typical Dutch Jew was traditional, little inclined to fanaticism, emancipated yet keeping largely to his own kind.

Above all, he was a loyal subject of the Dutch state," explains Socialist parliamentarian Judith C.E. Belinfante, a historian and the former director of Amsterdam's wonderful Jewish Historical Museum. Yet, tragically, it was this very sense of a "protected situation," insists Belinfante, that caused the "Jews of Holland to [tend] to be trusting of their government."

It was that trust that "blinded them to the real meaning of the restrictive measures now enacted by the Germans."

Not all Jews remained complacent. Young activists organized resistance within the Jewish quarter, and in February of 1941, non-Jewish workers staged a nationwide strike to protest Nazi brutality, especially in regard to Jews.

A furious Seiss-Inquart ordered the establishment of the Nazi-controlled Joodsche Raad, "Jewish Council" and on March 12 declared that Jews were not part of the Dutch people. The latter, he said, would have a clear choice: sympathy for the Jews or collaboration with the Germans.

In the summer of 1941, as in Austria in 1938, Jews were barred from public places in Holland, from transport, parks, swimming pools, theaters, and museums—in effect, from any contact with their gentile countrymen. Jewish children were barred from Dutch schools.

These isolating restrictions coincided with the first in a long series of heavy-handed confiscations of Jewish property. The first pack of vultures to descend on the Netherlands was the Einsatzstab Reichsleiter Rosenberg, the Rosenberg Special Operations Staff, named for Nazi Party ideological chief Alfred Rosenberg, to whom the Fuhrer had given a free hand to steal whatever he deemed necessary to promote the Nazi cause. In the Netherlands, this began with choice Jewish libraries, both public and private. Among the prizes plundered: the famed Rosenthal Collection of precious books.

As they would elsewhere, especially in France, the Nazis soon turned their attention to art and the noteworthy collections belonging to wealthier members of the Dutch-Jewish community. Hermann Goring himself made more than one trip to Amsterdam to visit the best dealers and collections and make his choices. Some of the art was legally purchased, if under duress and/or at bargain prices. But other works were simply confiscated, packed, and transported to Germany.

Later, Rosenberg's gang turned its attention to more mundane but no less lucrative prey: the household furniture and other belongings of Jews deported to the death camps. Dubbed "Aktion M"(for Meubel or furniture), it was an operation of staggering proportions. No sooner had a family been arrested and deported than one of a fleet of German-made trucks belonging to the Amsterdam-based Puls moving company would arrive and empty the apartment.

Says one Dutch Holocaust survivor, "If neighbors hadn't gotten there first."

According to Joseph Michman, author of "the Jewish community in Holland" "in a single year, 17,235 apartments were emptied of their contents, and loads totaling 16,941,249 cubic feet were crated and sent to Germany or to Eastern Europe to be divided among the ethnic German population being settled there."

"First," says Hague-born period scholar and Holocaust survivor, Professor Isaac Lipchits, himself a hidden child, "they took away our radios, then our bikes, our cars, our savings, our art, our furniture. Before we were deported, they even took our backpacks and wedding rings. And at Auschwitz they finally took the gold from our teeth. It was a demonic system."

"To organize and centralize this massive plunder, the Nazis established a highly specialized banking institution with main offices near the Amstel River just around the corner from the elegant Amstel Hotel. To "reassure" the Jews, they cynically named the depository "The Lippmann-Rosenthal & Co. Bank," the same name as that of a midsize, prewar Dutch-Jewish bank of impeccable reputation. In point of fact, the four-story redbrick building at 13 Sarphatistraat—which soon came to be popularly known as "Liro"—no longer had anything to do with the original bank or its Jewish founders. It had been seized from its Jewish owners in 1940 and given to a Nazi sympathizer as a prize for his loyalties to the Reich."

(Richard Chesnoff, *Pack of Thieves*)

"Had the two fine gentlemen who founded Lippmann-Rosenthal known what their bank came to be used for," says Isaac Lipchits, "they would still be spinning in their graves."

"To start the financial ball rolling, the Nazis first ordered all other Dutch banks to immediately transfer "known Jewish accounts" to the Liro. They followed in August 1941 by issuing Verordnung (Decree) 148/41, which blocked all Jewish-owned bank accounts and instructed all Dutch Jews not only to transfer their accounts and securities from other Dutch banks to the Liro but to deposit all cash holdings and checks of more than 1,000 guilders as well. The massive proceeds thus assembled were then to be turned over to the Vermoogensverwaltungs-und Rentenanstalt (Office of Property Administration and Pensions). It was this central German institute that administered the Liro's loot.

Jews were subsequently ordered to turn in gold and silver, jewelry, bonds, and insurance policies. Again Lippmann-Rosenthal was the central repository. By this time, the Nazis' Amsterdam bank was staffed with more than eighty Dutch employees, all drawn from respectable Dutch banks and other Netherlands financial institutions.

At first Jewish depositors were told they'd be allowed to withdraw up to 250 guilders per month per family of their own money from their Liro accounts. But this Nazi magnanimity soon ended..."

(Richard Chesnoff, *Pack Of Thieves*)

"The Liro," says Lipchits "became a bank where you could deposit but not withdraw."

Diamonds, the kind used for jewellery, is deemed important towards the German war effort, therefore many of the diamond workers involved in the business are given some special status. They do not initially have to report to be sent to the work camp Westerbork, because their jobs at home are more important to the war effort.

In 1942 it becomes a problem when many of them are targeted to be sent away. Therefore a list is composed so that anyone in the business can register and remain exempt from deportation.

A total of 1230 people register.

***

Daddy tells Mommy, "We are safe from deportation now since I registered as a diamond cutter." Mommy and Daddy dance around the kitchen. They are so happy.

***

After a while it becomes quite apparent that this is only a short-term goal and the quota is cut in half, and subsequently set aside all together.

***

Mommy and Daddy are whispering. I cannot hear what they are saying. Mommy starts to cry. I feel sad.

"Why is she crying?" I wonder.

Daddy yells, "It's the only solution, and this will save our children. It's too dangerous to bring them along. They will just slow us down."

Maurice stands in front of Daddy and looks up at him.

"Yes Daddy," he answers, "I will look after Jackie when you and Mommy are gone. Don't worry I am a big boy now."

He is only seven years old.

"Yes, I like the boys upstairs. They are my best friends," he says.

I think that's funny. He told me before that he did not like the boys.

Mommy is talking to me and Maurice now.

"Daddy and I are going away for a little while," she says, as tears are falling from her eyes. "Mrs. Vanderclooy, from upstairs, will look after you boys. We have left our things with her, my jewellery and my expensive china dishes. She will give them back once we come back from Switzerland. I have given her money for your food and other things. You'll be able to play with her two boys all the time"

"I want to go with you Mommy," I say with a whimper. "No, you can't Jackie"

"Mommy, I won't be bad anymore, I won't burn myself with milk anymore, I promise. Please, please. I'll be good from now on."

Mommy and Daddy are both crying and so not knowing what else to do, I cry too. Maurice is holding on to my hand, pushing back his tears. I think he does not want to cry in front of me because he is my big brother.

There is a knock on the door. It is my uncle Jules, Mommy's brother. He is wearing a German SS officer's uniform. Mommy and Daddy are surprised." Jules, where did you get the uniform?" daddy asks.

Uncle Jules says with a laugh, "I got it from the resistance people and they got it off a dead SS officer. They will help us get to Switzerland. They are giving us a car and a driver to get us to the border. Once at the border, another car will be waiting to take us all the way to France."

On a dark moonless night, a black car, with its lights turned off, pulls up in front of our house.

Mommy, Daddy and Uncle Jules, loaded down with bags, trudge down the flights of stairs.

Maurice and I stand near the car. We expect that we can go along for the long ride. I am quite excited, but as I look at mommy's face I notice that she is crying again.

I know that it is not a good sign. As I attempt to climb into the car, I can feel gentle hands restrain me.

"Mommy, you are squeezing me too hard, I can't breathe," I say, choking.

With jaws resolute, Mommy and Daddy get into the backseat and Uncle Jules takes a seat beside the driver. None of them turn around to look at me.

The car pulls away from the curb.

My big brother, Maurice, clutching my hand, is crying now. I can tell he wants to be courageous, but the burden of responsibility of looking after both of us, all by himself, appears to engulf him. We watch the car disappear into the night.

***

Dutch is a precise language. The word "biggelen" denotes the specific movement of a tear on a cheek. Singing at the top of one's voice is "volle borst" meaning full breast.

"The language of the Lowlands may also be the only one in the world with a specific verb for the systematic looting of a house: pulsen. It is derived from Abraham Puls & Sons, the name of the notorious Amsterdam moving-van company that Nazi-directed Dutch police employed to pillage and empty the homes of the 140,000 Jews of the Netherlands who were forced into hiding or shipped to their deaths during the Nazi occupation."

(Richard Chesnoff's, Pack of Thieves)

***

Mrs. Vanderclooy tells us to come in. We will be living with her from now on.

My tummy hurts and I feel like I'll throw up.

I whisper to Maurice,"I don't want to stay with her. I don't like her."

"I am your big brother, I'll protect you. I won't let anything bad happen to you. I promise," Maurice says.

Feeling a little better, I follow him to Mrs. Vanderclooy's flat. An uncertain future awaits us.

Mrs. Vanderclooy and some of her friends go to our flat and start to take items out.

"They won't need these anymore," one woman snickers, as she carries out a couple of chairs.

"You leave those alone, they're ours!" Maurice yells with a tone of indignation in his tiny voice.

Nobody pays any attention to us and continue to steal everything out of our house, until in the end there is nothing left but a pile of rubbish. We both stand around, shedding tears of anger and shame.

Mrs. Vanderclooy orders us in a sharp voice to come into her place. "Unless you want to spend the night on the landing," she adds with amusement. So with reluctance we enter Mrs. Vanderclooy flat.

"Mrs. Vanderclooy, Jackie, and I are hungry," Maurice begs.

"Sorry, your parents did not leave enough money for food for you two".

We watch, wide-eyed, as her two boys eat with gusto from their steaming plates of potatoes and carrots.

I smell the delicious scent of a freshly peeled orange. It makes my mouth water.

"Can I have a piece, Nikko?" I ask with excitement. Grinning, he hands me the orange peel. I am so hungry that I eat it. As I bite into the peel the bitter taste make me stop for a moment, realizing now that Nikko does not want to share the sweet fruit with me. I keep chewing on the peel. He and his brother Gerrit are laughing.

Nikko says,"Mom, Jackie is eating the orange peel. Is it not funny?"

Mrs. Vanderclooy looks at me as if I'm crazy. "What's the matter with you? Don't you know you have to eat the inside of the orange and not the outside?"

With a sense of triumph, Nikko stuffs the last piece in his mouth.

Mrs. Vanderclooy is not looking after Maurice and me at all. The money that Mommy gave her has bought lots of food for her and her boys, while Maurice and I only get little bits.

We go to bed hungry and we wake up hungry.

"Maurice I am hungry."

Maurice takes me out on the street in the morning to see if he can find something for us to eat. We walk by a grocery store and Maurice steals an apple. We run away as fast as we can. We did something bad, we stole. The storeowner watches us but he does not bother to run after us. After we turn the corner and out of danger, we each take a bite from the apple. It is the best apple we've ever eaten.

Somewhat full we look for things to do on the street.

Maurice whispers with a knowing look on his face, "Do you see all those people with a yellow star of David on their coats?" He points to a few with a sweeping motion of his arm. "They are Jews, you know. We don't have to wear a Star of David on our jackets, because with our blond hair and blue eyes, we don't look Jewish."

I am so glad about that, because if I had to wear a Star of David, I wouldn't know how to look Jewish.

The next morning the storeowner, standing outside his store, waits for Maurice and me to come around the corner.

Uncertain, we approach him, thinking that we are in big trouble. He'll probably beat us and want his apple back. Instead he gives us each another apple.

He says,"Please come by every day and I will give you something to eat. I don't want you two to go hungry. I know your Mommy and Daddy and I really like them.

He has tears in his eyes.

"If you're hungry just come here. You don't need to steal the food. I will give it to you."

Maurice is uncertain what to say. He is not used to much human kindness.

He stares at the man's kind face for a while and then says "Thank you for my brother and me."

The kind man mutters,"If it was not so dangerous for my family, I would look after you two myself."

CHAPTER 2

***

Terrible things are happening outside. At any time of night and day, poor helpless people are being dragged out of their homes. They're allowed to take only a knapsack and a little cash, and even then, they're robbed of these possessions on the way."

(Anne Frank, The Diary of Anne Frank, January 13, 1943)

***

I sit on the stoop outside the house. How did I get to this strange place? I feel very lonely. I wonder where Maurice is? Something bad must have happened to him, because he would never leave me by myself. I miss him so very much. "Boy is it ever cold." I can't get warm and I can't stop shivering. With no coat and just a thin sweater, the cold wind goes right through me and chills my skinny bony body. I watch as a fly walks in front of me, very slow. The fly must be cold too, because when I reach out for it, it does not try to fly away, I catch it very with no trouble. Fascinated by its strange behaviour I tug at its wings and then its legs. The fly buzzes around on its back for a while. Then I stick the fly in my mouth hoping this will stop the pain in my tummy. My clothes are chafing the burn scars on my arm and chest. It only hurts badly some of the time, not all the time.

I was in the big hospital for a long time where people were very cruel to me. They hurt me.

I walk around the sidewalk looking for something to eat; with a sense of triumph I peel a piece of chewing gum from the sidewalk. It does not have any taste.

Disappointed I go back in the house. Walking up the flight of stairs I hope the nice lady will let me back in this time. I bang on the door. Thank goodness, after a while, it opens, and the warm air in the flat feels good. Inside, the tallest man I have ever seen smiles down at me. I have to look way up to see his head. He pats me on the behind and gives me a candy. I love anything that is sweet. When I put it in my mouth it makes my mouth feel funny and watery. I make the candy last as long as possible by not sucking. It melts anyway until there is nothing left in my mouth.

The man says, in a deep voice, "My name is Hermann. What is your name, little man?"

"My name is Jackie."

The lady serves Hermann coffee and a cookie but she does not offer me one. Boy, I wish she would give me a cookie and a glass of milk. My mouth waters. I don't ask for one. Mommy always said to me: "Children that ask are passed over."

Hermann wears the biggest black boots I have ever seen. He has a shirt with a strange sign on his arm. I have seen that sign before, when the soldiers are marching in the street. He bounces me on his knee and says that he has a son my age at home. He finishes his coffee and cookie and then he gets up, puts on his heavy coat and hat. He thanks the lady. And then he is gone, leaving me alone with the strange lady.

The lady tells me I should call her Aunt Ninon and she says that we are at number ten Rue de l'Automne in Ixelles, near Brussels and she will look after me for a while. She is kind to me. I like her.

Aunt Ninon has a boy. His name is Raymond. He is eight years old. I do not like Raymond. He is mean and he makes fun of me. She also has a girl, and her name is Juliana. Juliana is a tiny baby. I like her. She is so tiny and she does not speak much. Juliana cries a lot though. It is dark outside now. Aunt Ninon has black paper in front of the windows so that nobody can look out. She has candles in the house and lights them with a match. The candles cast strange shapes on the walls. The shapes look like scary monsters.

Aunt Ninon puts me to bed in the front room. It is dark and cold in the room and I am scared to close my eyes. I can hear people talking in the front room, where it is nice and warm. I lie in bed facing the door because if I do not face the door someone will sneak up behind me and kill me. With my eyes open, I start to snore loudly so that they will think that I am sound asleep. The door opens and through slits in my eyes, I can see Aunt Ninon and Raymond approach the bed. Raymond yells "Boo" at the top of his voice, scaring me half to death. Then they laugh so hard that they make me laugh too. After that, I don't feel so scared anymore and even though my tummy still hurts I fall asleep.

Aunt Ninon's has a father and mother. They are nice people. I like them a lot. They say, "Call us Marain and Parain"

They bring me to a big church where they tell me that they take care of the cooking and the cleaning for the Catholic priests. The priests don't smile much and they mumble most of the time. I can't make out what they are saying.

Every time when Aunt Ninon has to take care of her business Marain and Parain take us along to the church. It is so very quiet in the church. "This is the house of God." Marain tells me. I love the house of God. It makes me feel that nothing bad will happen to me here. When you yell in the church, somebody answers back. I can't always understand what he says, but it is fun to speak with someone else. Nobody talks to me much. I yell" Hello" and he says"Hello". Parain laughs and says that it is called an echo; it's not really someone answering me.

The priests are wonderful and kind to us. They ask Marain and Parain if they would leave me and my brother at the rectory, which is next to the cathedral, so that they can make us into proper catholic boys. They make Maurice an altar boy and he helps the priests during the services. Maurice sings beautiful songs. Marain and Parain say "No, we can't leave these boys here because Ninon wants them back."

"After all" she says;"these are Jewish boys, not Catholics."

Feeling at peace and special, I love it when I go to the church, especially on Sundays when the big organ plays. The church is full of people. Moms and Dads come with their kids. Old ladies with coloured scarves on their heads and old men take off their hats when they come in. Mommy and Daddy would like it here. Every time I enter the church I dip my hand in water and then I cross myself and mumble something, because I see everybody else doing it. Marain nods with approval: "That's a good boy"

The boys sing beautiful songs. Their voices rise all the way up to the high ceiling. The pipes from the organ are so big that they take up the entire front wall off the church. I usually fall asleep after a while, when one of the priests stands up high in what Parain calls " the pulpit" and talks down to the people in a strange language.

Marain wakes me up and whispers; "Turn your chair around now so you can kneel down on the straw seat and rest your elbows on the back so you can pray like everyone else does." After a while my knees start to hurt. I tell Marain.

She says; "It's supposed to hurt." Mercifully, after a long time, and probably because God took pity on me and my sore knees, we can turn our chairs around again so that we can sit down. I try to understand what the priest says but I can't. Marain tells me that the priest speaks in Latin.

Maurice hands a cup to the priest and he drinks from it and then gives it back to him. Maurice says that he likes being an altar boy and he knows all the songs by heart. He sings along with the choirboys. I find it rather strange that the priest speaks in a language that no one understands. If he wants the people to know what God said he should speak in a language that people can understand.

I love Sunday afternoons. It is my favorite time because after the talk and the singing, when everyone else has left, we get to walk in the gardens behind the church. Brother Francois takes me for a walk and explains in a soft voice: "You see Jackie, there on the left; we have a vast area of vegetable gardens. We grow all our own food here, lettuce, cauliflower, tomatoes, peas, beans, carrots, onions, radishes, parsley and many other types of herbs as well as lots of potatoes. Oh yes, we love our potatoes. All kinds of animals can run free in that area to the right. We have chickens, rabbits, sheep and goats. See, way over there, is the pigpen. We keep it far enough away from our living quarters because pigs don't smell so good. Our pigeons are everywhere of course, they have their own house and we'll go and feed them if you want." All the pigeons gather around and there are so many flying around that I get scared. Then Brother Francois takes my hand and we continue on our wonderful adventure, "See here, past the vegetable gardens we maintain our botanical garden. Do you know what a Botanical garden is, Jackie?" I shake my head. "A botanical garden is a magical place. It's a place where we grow a wide variety of plants for ornamental purposes; we also have a library, a herbarium, an arboretum and greenhouses." I don't understand most of what he says but I nod as if I do. I don't want to disappoint him. This seems so important too him.

It is a beautiful sunny day. Some of the priests are in their shirtsleeves working in the vegetable garden. "Come and help us plant Jackie, we are planting radishes and carrots, beets and cauliflower today, and over there, and he points to an open spot you can plant these potatoes." He hands me a bag with potato peelings and a small shovel. Planting is hard work. I get thirsty. Marain comes out of the kitchen with a large pitcher of lemonade. We all stop planting for a moment of rest and Marain pours the lemonade in big glasses.

"Here Jackie since you've worked so hard you deserve a glass too" as she hands me one. Wishing this day would never end, I feel calm and happy in this house of God. Everybody calls it the house of God, but I haven't seen God anywhere yet, maybe he is hiding. I want to stay in this place forever.

For the first time in a long time, my tummy does not hurt. There is lots of food for everybody here. Marain heaps my plate up with meat, peas, potatoes, and lots of gravy. I have never had meat before. It is so good. She gives me a big glass of milk to drink. For dessert, she gives me a piece of apple pie. I never tasted anything so good. Marain lets me help her wash the dishes in the big sink. The sink is so big that I can sit and hide in it and nobody can see me. Just before bedtime, Marain fills the sink with warm water and she washes me. It feels so wonderful and warm. She puts on pajamas that are much too big for me and then she puts me to bed in a large bedroom, where there are many other beds.

I love Marain and Parain. Parain is the strongest man I know. He picks me up and lifts me over his head with one hand. He puts me on top of his shoulders and from there I can see the whole world.

CHAPTER 3

"Aunt Ninon can I have some water?" Sleepless and sweaty, my eyes are rolling back. She takes my temperature. It is 42 degrees Celsius. They rush me to the hospital in Schaerbeek.

The doctor examines me and says: "The boy has contracted dry Pleurisy, we'll have to keep him here for a while, and then looking at me; "we'll take good care of you."

I beg to go back home. "I won't be any trouble."

Aunt Ninon assures me that they will take good care of me at the hospital.

They are kind and gentle to me. Not like it was in the other hospital where I was always in pain. They put me in a room I share it with another little boy. He must be quite lonely because he cries a lot. My head hurts and I tell him to be quiet. He keeps on crying. I go over to his bed, I slap him, and I feel an indescribable feeling of power. He is quiet now. He has a game that I really like. You have to knock the pegs with a hammer until they come out the other side. One day I take his game and I tell him it is mine. I don't give it back to him and he cries.

He tells his parents, on the day that they visit, that I have taken his game. They come over to my bed and ask me if the game is mine.

Lying, I say; "Yes it is. My Mommy and Daddy gave it to me when I came to the hospital."

His parents tell him; "let him have the game."

I feel happy; I have never had my own game before.

A loud siren blears incessantly. We hear a gunshot then another.

I say to the boy in the next bed:"It must be St Nicholas coming."

A deafening sound and a blinding flash of light and then nothing.

I feel dizzy; I can't seem to open my eyes. I pull at the eyelids and my eyes open. Broken glass and stuff everywhere. I look for the boy in the next bed. I can't find his bed. The boy is on the floor with closed eyes. Is he dead? Everything is broken. It is very quiet now, not noisy like before. I lay very still and I feel wetness on my face and in my mouth. Funny, I am not in my bed, but instead I am lying on the floor in the middle of broken glass. Blood is coming out from many cuts in my head. Fire and smoke fill the room. It is hard to breathe the air. It bothers my throat and makes me cough. I am really scared. Will the flames burn me? Will I die? Is this what dying feels like? What is dying? I've heard Mommy and Daddy talk about death and dying.

The pain in my head is getting worse. Maybe if I don't move the pain will go away. It feels like I have been laying here for hours.

Men in black coats and big helmets arrive. One of them picks me up from the floor and carries me to another area of the hospital. "You'll be fine." is all he says, but somehow that's enough to make me feel safe in his strong arms. The shattered glass makes a crunching noise as the firefighter walks over it. The smoke is really thick. He puts a thing on my face and I can breathe better. He brings me to a small room and it is crowded with all kinds of people.

Doctors and nurses are looking after all the bleeding people. The fireman puts me down to sit on top of a warm radiator to await my turn for treatment. The radiator is hot and burns my bum, so I jump down. I have to stand around and wait. There are no beds and no chairs for me to sit on. After a long time, a man in a white coat comes over to me: "Well, let's have a look at you." The look on his face gives me a funny feeling in my stomach. He stares at a piece of metal that is stuck in the middle of my forehead. Glass is everywhere in my hair. The rest of my body is OK. Just my head is bleeding. The doctor looks at the piece of shrapnel in my forehead and he calls over the nurse:"Look; this piece of metal is perfectly centered in this boy's forehead and forms a perfect "V". The nurse shrugs and goes back to looking after one of the many other people.

The piece comes out pretty quick as he pulls at it. It does not hurt and it does not bleed much. He has a curved needle and black tread and sticks the needle in my forehead. Now a nurse is pulling at the pieces of glass in my hair. After having removed all the pieces, she washes my head with some red stuff. It really stinks. The doctor takes his needle and tread and starts stitching my head. I can feel the needle go in. It hurts a lot, but I do not cry. After the doctor is finished with the needle she wraps my head with white bandages. She goes around and around until I no longer recognize myself. The doctor gives me a needle. My head no longer hurts and they put me in a nice clean bed. I am so very tired that I fall asleep right away.

After many days, aunt Ninon picks me up from the hospital. We take a taxi home. She says; "You're all better now, but I will have to change the bandages from time to time". That scares me because it hurts when she pulls the bandages off.

CHAPTER 4

Today is October 12 1944. It's your birthday today is it not?" asks aunt Ninon.

"Yes" I answer, not knowing what she is talking about. "You are four years old now; we'll have to make you a birthday cake". The thought of sweet gooey cake makes my mouth water.

Uncle Jules arrives. I haven't seen him for a very long time. When he comes home he makes me happy because he brings me some candy. I run over to meet him, but then I stop. He looks at me with a very sad face and he says nothing. He talks to aunt Ninon in hushed tones. She cries now. What happened? I don't understand it. I try to think what I did wrong. I cannot think of anything. Unless she cries because I peed in my bed before. Yes, that's probably it. I sit as quietly as possible now so that I do not attract attention to myself. Then she comes over to me and pulls me to her and holds me for a long time, all the time mumbling: "It's going to be OK; it's going to be OK. We'll look after you and your brother. We promised."

CHAPTER 5

When Maurice is around, which is not very often, he and I sleep in the same bed? I like sleeping with Maurice. His body is nice and warm and he holds on to me so that I feel that nothing can get me now. Sometimes I get worried though, because he breathes very loudly as he cannot seem to get enough air in. He chokes and coughs. Aunt Ninon says that he has asthma.

Aunt Ninon always yells at him, because she says he dirties the pillow case from the snot that comes out of his nose at night. She says that he has to sniff up warm water with salt up his nose. He does it, he always listens to her and he wants to make her happy. She is never happy with him. I don't think she likes him very much. This makes me so very sad that I cry. Doesn't she know he's my brother? She puts him in an orphanage in Wezenbeek. I want to go and visit but I do not know where Wezenbeek is. I wish Mommy and daddy were here. They would know where the orphanage is and they would take me to see him.

CHAPTER 6

~

When Maurice and I are together he tells me about some of the things that happened to him while he spent time in different orphanages. He does not like orphanages and he runs away from them all the time.

Maurice tells me: "One day the German soldiers came to the orphanage and lined up all the kids so that they could take our blood. The German blood supply was running low for the soldiers that are fighting at the front. So one after the other we are taken into a room and blood is taken from us. While we stand in line waiting to go into the room, I and a few other kids decided that, if we could, we would run away. Just as it is my turn to give blood the German doctor said that they have taken enough blood for the day.

They told me I'll be first in line the following morning.

Many of the children died that night. That night we decided to run away, me and three other boys and an old rabbi. Very early the next morning, under the cover of darkness, we decided to escape. I didn't know where the old rabbi came from, but all of a sudden he was there. He took charge of us. We ran for hours until we got to a farm where we hid in the barn. We were really hungry and ate some of the straw. One of the boys got very sick after eating the straw. I held on to comfort him and he died in my arms. I got very upset. The farm lady found us and although she yells at us, gave us some food to eat. She let us stay for a few days but then she told us that it was too dangerous for us to stay there and that eventually we'd be discovered by the Germans.

The Maquis (Belgian resistance fighters) come at night and took us to a different orphanage. This one was run by the nuns. It was suppertime and they served us our meals. Potatoes and vegetables and a large piece of meat. I asked one of the nuns what kind of meat it was and she said that it was pork. I told her that because I was Jewish I could not eat pork and that if I eat the pork would make me sick. She wallops me in the head and tells me to eat anyway. I took the piece of meat, secretly, and stuck it in my pocket. When I went outside I threw it away."

This story is one of a very few that he told me. He is until now, he is presently sixty nine years old, unable to share the horrendous experiences from his early childhood during the war. The memories overwhelm him. Many a night, he tells me, he will wake up in a cold sweat, hyper ventilating, haunted by the sound of heavy boots coming down the hall and then, men in uniforms, breaking down the door and dragging him out.

One day I hope he will be empowered to share his tragic childhood experiences with the rest of the world.

***

Too bad that Maurice is not with me very often. I feel sad and lonely when he is gone. I miss him and Mommy and Daddy terribly. When will they come back to get us? Nobody knows.

CHAPTER 7

~

Dost Thou wail, or shall I wail? Rather shall I weep at the
fewness of Thy champions, O Thou Who hast caused the
wailing of the worlds...
Baha'u'llah, *Fire Tablet.*

When I asked Koos Smoor why his parents, Gerrit and Toos
(Antonia Wilhemina) endangered their own lives and their children's
lives by hiding Jews, he shrugged, a sort of a Gaelic shrug, and
responded; "they knew it was the righteous thing to do."

"You mean it is the Christian thing to do?"

"Look" He replies with a bit of an edge; "Gerrit, my father,
was a member of "de Sociaal Democratisch Arbeids Partij" (SDAP)
(Social Democratic Workers Party) and an avowed atheist. Call him
a humanist, if you want to label him. To leave anyone in harms way,
Jew or not, was unthinkable in his mind. He and Toos would not be
able to look each other in the eye if they abandoned someone in that
fashion. It just was not an option."

The answer evokes the true humanity in man and is so noble
that it makes me cry.

CHAPTER 8

***

There is a lady that lives one floor below Aunt Ninon's. She is visiting us today. This is the first time I have seen her at Aunt Ninon's. Usually we visit her. She has difficulty walking and likes to stay in her own place. Her name is Madame Gaston. When I knock at her door she asks me to come in and gives a cup of cocoa.

She is a very nice old lady. Her hair is gray and she has it tied into a bun, just like Mommy does, except Mommy's hair is not the same colour.

Aunt Ninon is talking about Uncle Jules to the lady. She says that the Gestapo has taken him to a work camp called Breendonk. That is a bad place where they make people work very hard. The Gestapo is very mean to the people.

***

Breendonk is located along the ancient highway from Brussels to Antwerp. Breendonk was a military fort and the buildings were built using concrete, at the beginning of the twentieth century. The Germans use Breendonk as a holding camp designed to receive Jews and political prisoners before they are transferred to Auschwitz.

***

"They beat Jules." she says to Madame Gaston. She sounds very upset.

"Jules is a barber by profession and they let him cut hair and shave the beards of the German officers in the camp. He was allowed to move around the camp freely, cutting the hair of "Les sales Boches" as well as some of the prisoners. One day, while he was shaving someone, he feigned a seizure and cut the man's throat. They beat Jules and he is pretty badly hurt. I must go to Breendonk to look after him the Gestapo told me. They also want to ask me questions about Maurice and Jackie. Les Boches, they know everything. How did they know about the boys?"

I am scared; we did not do anything bad. Why are they talking so softly? I can barely hear. Aunt Ninon says something about hiding Jews. Madame Gaston shakes her head and says "absolutely not!"

"Jackie, you must leave this place." She tells me in a gentle voice. "I already made arrangements for Maurice. He is in a safe place in an orphanage. With his blond hair and blue eyes nobody knows that he is a little Jewish boy. But you, you are too young to be in an orphanage. You will be staying with some people I know, friends of mine, in Holland. A car will pick you up in the morning. It is just too dangerous for you to stay here, with me gone."

"Auntie, I can stay with Marain and Parain."

"No, you cannot mon cheri, Juliana and Raymond are staying with them and with you there also it will be far too many in the small house."

In the morning I have to leave aunt Ninon's house. I do not want to go. I like it here. Aunt says that she will be gone for a while; therefore she won't be able to look after me. She kisses me on the cheek and makes the sign of the cross with her finger on my forehead.

"Que Dieu te béni." she whispers

Juliana and Raymond are being picked up by Marian and Parain.

"Why can't I go there too?" I ask

"They only have a small place and there is not enough room for you. I already told you that. And anyways, they don't want to take a chance to hide you. It is just too dangerous." she answers.

A man from the Resistance knocks at the door and after Aunt Ninon and he talk for a while he takes me by the hand and we walk down the stairs. I don't look up to see if Aunt Ninon is watching me. I feel sad and angry that she is sending me away. I've been sent to so many different places so many times, that I don't cry anymore. The man opens the car door and he puts me inside, beside him. We drive for a long time. Once into the countryside I see animals eating grass. I have never seen those kinds of animals before. They have different colours. There are many different animals.

"What kind of animals are those?" I ask him

He seems happy enough to be able to talk: "Those are horses" pointing to some of the animals. "And over there, you see those animals that are black and white? Those are cows. They give us milk."

We don't talk much after that. But that's OK with me; I like to be quiet, it lets me think.

Everything is so green. The car drives on a road and there are trees on both sides of the road. The branches of the trees touch each other at the top. So that it looks like we are driving along in a big green room. It is a warm day. I like the feeling of the sun shining on my face. I am happy to be outside. At Aunt Ninon's I could not go outside often. We had to stay in the house most of the time.

We are not driving in the green room anymore. When I look up I can see the sky again. The sky is so blue. I see birds flying. Small birds and bigger ones. The big ones are black. I can't tell the colour of the smaller birds. I've never really noticed birds before. With my head back resting on the back of the seat, I can keep looking up and not get tired. The birds flap their wings and suddenly change direction in midair. How can they do that? I wish I could fly. If I was up there with the birds, I could look down and look for Mommy and Daddy. Maybe I could see them. Why did Mommy and Daddy leave us? Oh, how I miss them. I miss Mommy touching me on my cheek and holding me in her arms so safe and warm. No bad things could ever happen in Mommy's arms. I better stop thinking like that, because I want to cry now and I can't cry in front of this man. He would look at me in a funny way and he would make fun of me.

If the birds can fly why can't I? They make it look so easy. Now I am looking into the sun. I can't stand it for long; I have to close my eyes. I fall asleep.

The road is very bumpy and shakes me so hard I wake up. How long did I sleep for? The driver had to pull off the road to let a large bunch of trucks and tanks pass.

"If anyone comes over and asks you a question, don't answer. Just let me do all the talking." He whispers. I just nod.

The soldiers and their trucks take up the whole road. Many of the soldiers are walking along beside the trucks their rifles hang over one of their shoulders, and some of the soldiers are sitting in the back of the trucks and some of the soldiers are riding alongside on bicycles. I remember, a long time ago, when I saw the soldiers before, in Amsterdam, with Daddy; they seemed to walk different, together, in large rows. The loud noise they made with their boots scared me. Now they don't make that noise anymore. I can just hear the loud sound of the truck engines. A horse pulls a big cart with a large gun on it; some soldiers are lying down in the back of the cart, on top of bags, with their eyes closed. Some of the soldiers look at us as they walk by, but nobody comes over to talk to us. Once everybody passed and the road is quiet again. the driver drives his car back on the road and we continue the long drive to Holland.

We arrive at a large house. The driver stops the car.

"This is where you will be staying." He takes out my suitcase and gives it to me. "Good luck." He says as he drives off. He does not shake my hand, no hug, no smile. A lady comes out of the house and hugs me like I was her long lost son. I've never seen the lady before.

"I've been expecting you. Your Auntie told me you were coming. I am friends with her and your Uncle Jules. Are you hungry?

"Yes." I haven't had anything to eat since we left this morning. "I have to pee very badly." I add with a feeling of shame. The lady shows me where the bathroom is. "Do you need any help?" She asks with a smile.

"No, thank you."

She seems very friendly and pretty. As she walks her skirt makes a noise, swish, swish it goes. She has red lips and her cheeks have red spots on them, just as if she used paint. When she comes closer to me I can smell her. She smells really, really good

She makes me a plate of warm milk with sugar and bread in it. She calls it pap. I watch her as she puts everything together. I don't say anything and she doesn't either, but from time to time she looks at me and smiles and I can see her white teeth.

"You'll be safe with me." is all she says.

She pours the pap in a bowl and puts it in front of me where I am sitting, at the kitchen table. With her free hand she gives me a spoon.

"Can you eat by yourself?"

"I am five years old. I always eat by myself" I answer. What does she think that I am a little boy?

The pap tastes wonderful and sweet. I've never eaten anything so good.

"Can I have some more?

"Why of course you can, little boy." And she pours more of the wonderful pap in my plate.

"I am not a little boy."

"Sorry, I know you are a big boy. You've been on your own for such a long time." She murmurs, with tears in her eyes.

"It's such a lovely day, do you want to go for a walk?" she asks.

"Yes." Nobody except Maurice ever takes me for walks. But with Maurice we were always looking for things to eat. It is warm. We left our coats in the house. We walk. She holds me by the hand. I feel safe. There are many other people walking. Daddies and Mommies walk, arm in arm, and their children jumping and skipping ahead of them, being yelled at from time to time to be careful. It is such a beautiful day.

When we get back home, she undresses me and we go for a nap. Exhausted from the long ride I fall asleep immediately. She lies down with me. Someone is touching my dickie. It grows and I wake up. Her touching hands and mouth feel good. Suddenly I am on top of her, my head resting on her bare breasts and her legs are wrapped around me. I feel warm and wet inside her embrace. I close my eyes. I wish I could stay there forever.

CHAPTER 9

I awaken and I feel very hot. The lady puts a thermometer in my behind.

"You have a temperature of 41°." she says, with a sound of worry in her voice. I better take you to the hospital."

"Oh, I have had this before. It's nothing. I don't want to go to the hospital."

After she has put my clothes on, she carries me most of the way to the hospital because I am far too weak to walk. I am so dizzy. At the hospital she puts me in a chair and tells me to wait. She runs to get a nurse: "Nurse, nurse, I have a sick little boy over there. Please help me."

The nurse says: "Please wait your turn. We have many sick little boys."

I remember that when I was in other hospitals, I had to wait a long time before someone would look after me. The room is spinning. I close my eyes and fall asleep.

A doctor takes my shirt off and he holds this thing against my chest that is attached to his ears. It feels cold.

"This boy has pneumonia. He'll have to be hospitalized. This time I don't hate to be in the hospital. I fall asleep again. Every time I wake up, people with concerned faces are looking at me and fuss over me, and then I fall asleep again. As I wake up this time the people no longer have sad looks on their faces.

The nurse says: "You were asleep for a very long time. Your fever has broken and you can eat some food now".

Many people come and visit me now. They tell me that they are my aunts and uncles. I don't remember ever having seen them before.

They are very happy; they say:"While you were asleep, the Krauts surrendered and the war is finally over. The monsters have fled. The nightmare is over." I am very happy too because Maurice wanted the war to be over. I still don't know what war is.

"Where are my Mommy and Daddy?"

Nobody answers.

***

With the war over "The evil continued well beyond the destruction of the third Reich and the end of Europe's World War II. Newly liberated nations like France and The Netherlands conveniently absorbed into their own governmental coffers much of what remained from the Nazi loot. Few made any intense effort-or any effort at all- to find the heirs of the victims.

Nor was it only the conquering and conquered who took advantage of the slaughter years that decimated Europe's Jewry. A lofty policy of neutrality enabled the national and private financiers of Switzerland, Sweden, Portugal, Spain, Argentina and other non-combatants to trade with both Axis and Allies and reap enormous profits in the process- not the least of them from the laundering of the tons of gold the Nazis had looted from the vaults of the nations they conquered or torn from the ring fingers and teeth of the victims they slaughtered.

(Richard Chesnoff, *Pack of Thieves*, pge 2)

***

CHAPTER 10

The liberation of Holland cost the lives of over 50,000 Allied soldiers. Altogether 4,500 Dutch soldiers died for their country, as did 258 POWs who died in German prison camps. At sea, a total of 1,500 Dutch sailors lost their lives and 110,000 Dutch Jews were exterminated. Some 23,000 citizens died in air raids...Executions and massacres claimed over 2,800 victims, 19 of whom were women. In all, 237,300 Netherlanders perished during the Nazi occupation. This does not include the 10,000 Dutch pro-Nazis who died fighting on the German side.

About 25,000 Dutchmen were pro-nazi and fought for Germany. Around 10,000 of them were killed during the war and although many fought bravely on the Allied side, it is a sad fact that more went into battle wearing the field grey uniform of the enemy than in the British khaki.

The loot the Germans transported back to the Reich from Holland was staggering:

- 13,786 metal working machines
- 2,729 textile machines
- 18,098 electric motors
- 358 printing presses
- 31 dredgers
- Over 7,000 barges
- 90,000 lengths of railway line and a half million sleepers
- Over 60,000 motor cars, 40,000 trucks and 25,000 motor bikes
- 154,647 kilos of Dutch gold disappeared into the Reich bank's safes in Berlin
- 320,000 cows, 472,036 pigs and 114,220 horses.

A total of 346 works of art were also stolen including 27 Rembrandts, 12 Hals, 47 Steens, 40 Rubens, and 12 Van Goghs. Most of these paintings were recovered after the war. Sadly only a few were returned to their original owners. No great effort was made by the Dutch authorities to locate the rightful heirs of these priceless works of art http://members.iinet.net.au/~gduncan/1944.html#lesser_known_1944

CHAPTER 11

"Ah, peace" Everyone is so happy. They slap each other on the back and they smile. "Isn't fantastic we got rid of the Huns? We don't have to be afraid ever again. Thanks to the Canadians. The Canadians are so wonderful. Nice young boys and so polite too."

I still don't understand war and now I am told that we are at peace. Life is confusing. Life is not much different now than before. The only difference; I don't have to hide anymore. Nice people come to take me home with them. They promise I can stay at their house for a while. Never having stayed anywhere for very long it feels good to rest in one place for a time. Auntie Saar is Mommy's sister and Uncle Jonas is Daddy's brother.

"Why are Mommy and Daddy not here to pick me up?"

"They could not come. That is why they asked us to pick you up." They brought me some new clothes.

"Here try these on," auntie Saar says. The clothes almost fit. The shirt and pants are a few sizes too large.

"They're just fine because you'll grow in to them."

I am not sure what that means.

Uncle Jonas has a flower store. He and his family live in Bussum and his store is called "Bloemenhuis Veffer" They have six children. Shelley and Japie, Meipie, Jopie, Jultje and Appie. Appie and Meipie are always fighting with each other. Auntie Saar says: 'Say hi. These are all your cousins."

Auntie Saar speaks of the family's time in hiding, "We were hidden for over 1000 days. All of us were hidden in a tiny, airless room with no windows. The entrance into the room was hidden behind a large Armoire. We could not make any sound and no one could go out for fear that we'd be discovered and taken by the Germans and sent to a concentration camp. Thank God we managed to survive this ordeal and we were all saved. It was a dangerous time for us as well as for the family that hid us. If discovered it would have meant certain death for us all. The family that kept us hidden for all that time is the real heroes of the war. We'll be forever grateful." She cries and hugs her kids like a mother hen trying to gather them all around her.

Shelley plays the accordion. She plays "stormy weather' and "don't fence me in" She sings me a song. "Alle eendjes zwemmen in het water, (all the ducks are swimming in the water) Falderalderira, falderalderara, Alle eendjes zwemmen in het water falfal falfalderalderiefaldera. I love that song.

"Sing it again Shelley." After a few more times she says: "That's enough, it's time for you to go bed young man. You are still sick and you need your rest" She puts on a pair of pajamas. I don't know who's they are. I know they're not mine. They have stripes running up and down in blue and white. The sleeves are way too long and she rolls them up and the pant legs are also too long and I trip over them, flat on my face. She laughs. It's good to hear her laugh.

My bedroom is on the third floor of the house. It's pretty boring up there, all by myself, with nothing to do all day. The walls are covered with wallpaper with coloured designs. One corner of the wallpaper is torn. I wonder who did that. Whoever did it must have gotten in real big trouble. I count the different colours. One, two, three, four. What comes after four? I'm not sure. I see two more colours after four. The designs are all the same, no matter where I look. I start to see double, so I look up at the ceiling. Thank goodness there is nothing on the ceiling. It's blue, like the sky outside. I'm so bored. No one comes upstairs except Shelley. She brings me food and refreshments. The boys are playing some kind of game. I can hear them; they make a lot of noise. Curious to see what they are doing I decide to get up to look out the window. I throw back the covers and step down on the floor. I don't watch where I step and my foot gets stuck in the pisspot, beside the bed. I forgot it was there. Silly me,

I should have remembered. I used it enough times. The pisspot tips over. It makes a clanging noise. Shelley comes running up the stairs and I know I'm in for it now. Better get my story straight:

"It's an accident, Shelley, honest. My foot is all wet."

"That's what happens when you don't listen. I told you to stay in bed." Shelley is really mad. She thinks I did it on purpose.

"Shelley, please don't be mad at me, it was an accident." Maybe if I repeat it a second time she'll believe me.

I hate it when Shelley is mad at me. She'll probably send me away now. She stomps out of the room to empty what was left in the pisspot.

"Stay in bed, don't you dare come out, I'm going to get some rags to clean up this mess." A while goes by and when she returns she's all happy again, as if nothing happened and she is humming a song as she cleans up the mess. I look at her from my bed, not sure what to think of the situation. Will she start yelling again or did she really forget what I did?

"Jackie, I can't be mad at you, after all you've been through, you poor boy." And a tear trickles down her cheek.

I feel better. I don't like people yelling at me.

Shelley is really pretty and she has a boyfriend. I have watched them when they are together and they kiss a lot. They think they are alone but I can see them from behind the chair, but they can't see me. I get a pain in my leg and I come out from my hiding place.

"Jackie, come and say hi to Martie Stern, he is a Canadian soldier. Did you know that the Canadian soldiers liberated Holland?" I nod, not really knowing for sure what liberated means.

Martie speaks different. I cannot understand anything he says. Martie has a friend that is also a soldier. His name is Earl. They both stay at the armoury. The armoury is a place where soldiers live and it is right next door to Uncle Jonas' flower store. I am standing on the wall in front that goes all around the armoury and Earl is holding on to me tightly. He gives me his package of cigarettes to hold.

He says: "These are Exports." Shelley takes our picture with me holding up the green package of Exports. Earl is kind to me.

"I want to smoke just like you Earl." He thinks it's funny and laughs. Everyone is standing outside now; Uncle Jonas, Shelley, Martie, Auntie Saar.

"You want to smoke, I'll give you a cigarette" says Uncle Jonas and he gives me a rolled up piece of white paper. I stick it in my mouth and he lights it with his lighter. It nearly burns my nose. I guess I am still too small to smoke.

Uncle Jonas smokes Schimmelpenninck cigars; they smell good. He gives me the band from the cigar and I put it on my finger. It looks just like a real ring.

Earl always has candies or chocolates in his pocket. He gives me a Hershey bar. I don't like any other food, but I sure love candies and chocolates. Maurice and I know where they keep the chocolate bars in the Jeeps. So at night, when it's dark, we sneak out and we go look in the map compartments of the Jeeps and take the chocolate bars. All the kids in the neighborhood seem to know the hiding place for the chocolate bars. But that's OK, every night there are more for everybody. All the people love the Canadian soldiers. Everybody cheers, wave flags and smile when they see them. Excited to see them too, I run across the street to get a better view, not watching both ways, when I cross the street, a bike knocks me down and runs over me. My knee and my head hurt. Japie comes quickly to where I fell and carries me back into the house. Shelley puts a bandage on my head. My head is bleeding. Auntie Saar tells me to lay still. I am happy about that because I am sooo dizzy.

CHAPTER 12

The war ended only a little while ago and Shelley and Marty tell her parents that they want to get married. Marty has to go back to Canada and Shelley says that she will go with him once they are married.

When the wedding day arrives, I am really excited. I have never been to a wedding. The whole family has come out to celebrate. There is Auntie Bora, her husband and their son Harry, Auntie Roo, Uncle Levie and Loekie, Judith and Jopie Dinsdag, Auntie Miep and Uncle Louis, Auntie Ninon and Uncle Jules, but my Mommy and Daddy did not come.

"Where are my Mommy and Daddy Shelley?

"Oh, they could not be here today. They had something else important." She answers with a sad look in her eyes. I guess she must be sad because they are missing her fun wedding. She looks so pretty in her wedding dress and Marty is so handsome in his top hat and tails. I get to ride with them in a beautiful carriage pulled by a horse. The carriage has a pink bow at the back of it and flowers, pink and white ones all over. Even the horse looks happy, probable because he has white feathers on him. A man sitting in the front of the carriage is telling the horse where to go. He pulls on the straps that are attached to the horse's mouth. I wonder if he is hurting the horse. We arrive at a wonderful garden. Shelley says: "This is where I am getting married." She points to a white tent. She calls it the Chuppah.

"Shelley what is a Chuppah?"

"It is a wedding canopy at a Jewish wedding, sweetie. See it is held up by four poles with white fabric stretched over top of it and Marty and I will stand under it in front of the rabbi"

"In case it rains, then you won't get wet, right?"

"No silly it's Jewish tradition. Now be a dear and go sit on Auntie Miep's lap so that you'll be able to see the wedding better. She is right over there. The ceremony is starting right now."

I walk across the white carpet to where auntie Miep is and she picks me up. Shelley is right I can see everything from up here. Auntie Miep puts a white hat on my head.

"What did you that for Auntie?"

"That's a keppeltje. You have to wear it out of respect for God. In front of him you must always cover your head"

"Where is he auntie? I can't see him anywhere."

"Shhh. The wedding is starting."

The ceremony starts and people are walking from the back of the garden to the Chuppah. So many people, I can't count them all. And then Shelley comes walking down, holding on to her Daddy's arm. She smiles, everybody looks at her. She stops under the Chuppah and stands beside Marty. Now the rabbi tells her to walk around Marty a whole bunch of times. Around and around she goes. She must be getting dizzy.

Auntie Miep whispers in my ear: "Jackie, watch, now the rabbi will marry them." The rabbi talks, but I don't understand a word he says.

"What's he saying Auntie."

"He's reciting a blessing about the sanctity of married life." I nod but I don't understand. There are so many things I don't understand. The bride and groom drink wine. The rabbi mumbles some more things and then Marty stamps his foot on the floor and everybody yells: "Mazel Tov." We all clap it is such a happy occasion and everybody is smiling.

"Where are my Mommy and Daddy auntie Miep?"

"They could not come. They had something else to do."

"What can be more important than the wedding Auntie?"

"I don't know dear. Whatever it is must be mighty important to keep them away from this gassene."

"Auntie what is gassene?"

"That's a Yiddish word for wedding, dear."

She hugs me so tight I gasp for air.

Shelley and Marty look so happy. Everybody wishes them Mazel Tov and a long and happy life together. Soon they will go to Canada to live.

Some men are now playing different things I have not seen before and, together they make sweet music. Marty dances with Shelley, so close. Other people dance too. Auntie Miep takes me by both hands and twirls me around until I'm dizzy. We all eat wedding cake. It tastes very sweet. The party lasts a long time. People act silly, they sing and dance and drink wine. Exhausted I fall asleep on somebody's knee. Someone carries me upstairs to my room, undresses me and puts me into bed.

"Goodnight sweet little boy. God willing your parents will return."

CHAPTER 13

When the family sits down at the table to eat supper, Auntie Saar tells me to sit down. "Over there," she points to an empty chair, next to Shelley. Right away I get a funny feeling in my tummy and as soon as Shelley puts something in my mouth it stays there. The food won't go down.

"Swallow it" she says. I swallow and the food comes right back up all over the table. Every time I eat the same thing happens. I retch and the food falls out of my mouth. I can't help it.

"Let's take him to see the doctor tomorrow". Shelley suggests. After the doctor pokes me with different things he is quiet for a long time. Then he says: "Jackie is malnourished. He did without food for such a long time that now his body rejects it. The problem is more psychosomatic than it is physical. A stay at the sanatorium in Laren will do him a world of good."

"I don't understand, Doctor. When we give him cake, chocolates and candies he has no trouble eating. Only when he eats real food."

"That is the psychosomatic part of the condition. His brain does not see candy or cake as food. He cannot survive on that kind of food. He needs nourishing things" answers the doctor.

"A sanatorium is a place where people go when they have been very sick. You'll be better before you know it" Shelley explains.

"I don't want to go to a sanatorium."

"It'll be OK. You'll see."

Uncle Jonas and auntie Saar drive me to Laren the following day.

"I don't want to stay here: I want to go home with you."

They kiss me and leave. Feeling abandoned and alone I cry very loud. Nobody pays any attention. I cry louder. A man in a white coat comes; he takes down the bed covers and starts to hit me on my bare bottom. It hurts so badly. After a while, it does not hurt anymore. He tells me to be quiet; otherwise, he will beat me again. Now I am as quiet as a little mouse. Nobody talks to me here, just the nurse when she comes and takes my temperature says "good morning." Nobody ever comes to visit. When it is sunny outside, someone will roll my bed into the garden. It is warm. I can smell the flowers. Blue, white, yellow, red and other colours I don't know all the names. There are so many, I can't count them. The air outside smells fresh. Inside it stinks. I can breathe the cool air all the way in. It feels good.

The nurse comes over after a while and says: "It's time to go in for lunch. You must be really hungry after breathing all this fresh air." I am not hungry. When they put food in my mouth my stomach feels funny, and I have to throw up. Every meal is the same. They put a tube down my throat and into my stomach.

"That feels awful. Please don't do that anymore," I beg.

"Well, then eat," the man in the white coat says.

"I can't eat. I am not hungry."

They keep putting the tube in my throat. It really hurts and I can hardly swallow now. Auntie Saar and Uncle Jonas come and visit me.

The doctor says; "There is nothing more we can do for Jackie. His body is healthy now. The reason he cannot eat is not physical it's mental. Because he has not eaten regularly for such a long time, his brain tells his body he has no need for food. He will have to re-learn how to eat." I don't understand what he means.

"He can go home with you, we'll do up the discharge papers." The doctor walks out the room leaving me with Auntie Saar and Uncle Jonas.

"Jackie, You are a big boy now, you are almost six years old and we are taking you to a farm that is not very far from the here."

"I want to go home with you. Please let me come home with you."

"No, we can't Jackie, we have six children of our own There is barely enough food for them. Let alone for you and your brother Maurice"

"I won't eat auntie, honest."

From the way she talks though, I can tell she is not going to change her mind, so I stop talking to them.

CHAPTER 14

After we leave, a short distance away from the hospital we arrive at this big house with a white fence around it.

"This is where your Aunt Dora and Uncle Kees Bijl live. They will take good care of you" Auntie Dora comes over to me, she is fat, she grabs, and hugs me in her big arms. I don't like to be grabbed and hugged. Then she kisses me, which I don't like either. Uncle Kees is skinny. He puts out his hand. I don't know what to do. I think he knows something is wrong and he takes my hand and start to pump my arm up and down, until my arm feels like its going to fall off. All the while Uncle Kees has a great big grin on his face. I think I like these people.

Uncle Jonas pinches my cheek; "Jackie, you be a good boy now and eat all your food. OK? They both kiss me and after saying goodbye to everyone they leave me.

Auntie Dora pats me on the behind "Have you ever seen chickens and rabbits?" she ask me "We have all kinds of different farm animals here. Come I'll show you." She holds the gate open for me and we go into what she calls the courtyard.

"I've seen chickens and rabbits and goats and pigs at the church that Marain and Parain always took me to. They also had pigeons. Do you have pigeons here?"

"No. Sorry no pigeons. But I bet they did not have cows at the church. We have Holstein cows here. They give us wonderful milk. Would you like a glass of fresh milk, Jackie?"

"Yes, please, that would be nice." They let me drink it straight from the cows utter. That what Aunt Dora calls it. It's very good and creamy. She squeezes the utters one at the time. The milk squirts into the pail and before long the pail is full of milk. "Here you try it." She says. No matter how hard I squeeze no milk comes out. She puts her hand over mine as I squeeze and the milk comes out again. I sit on a three legged stool. After she helps me she lets go and I continue to milk and now I can manage it on my own. The cows are all milked and I feel good that I was able to do it on my own. It was a lot of work.

Uncle Kees asks:"Do you want to help me make butter?"

"Yes". I watch him as he puts milk in a long round pot. He has a big stick that comes out of the pot in the top and he starts to move it up and down. He lets me do it. It is hard work. He calls it churning. At first it's pretty easy. The stick goes up and down without much trouble. After a while it gets pretty hard, I get very tired and I can't do it anymore. He finishes it off.

"You want to taste some butter. Come on with me in the kitchen and we'll put some of this fresh butter on a nice piece of bread for you. I bet you've never tasted anything this good in your life." In the kitchen he cuts a thick piece of brown bread and spreads butter all over it. He gives it to me and when I bite into it I think he is right. I have never tasted anything this good. Ever.

"Yummy, this is so good," Uncle. "I am glad to be here I hope I never have to leave." I still have trouble eating my food but when I eat little bits of food I don't get sick in my tummy. I still don't like eating though; Aunt Dora is nice, because she never forces food into my mouth. She lets me eat on my own. They have no children of their own. I think they should have some, because they are so kind and gentle. I have my own room. I don't have to share my bed with anybody. It's a big room with a big white bed and a thick cover on the bed. When I crawl into it at night I can hide and nobody can see me. But I can see them. The windows have curtains with flowers on them. The walls have wallpaper and I count the different designs of the wallpaper. At night the designs change shape and they look like big bad people. I am afraid at night in the dark. When I get too scared I hide under the covers. And auntie leaves the bedroom door open and the light in the hall is on. It makes me feel safe.

It's very quiet here, not like at Auntie Saar's. At Auntie Saar's there were many people all the time. All were talking at the same. Some were yelling very loud. I don't like the yelling and I hold my hands over my ears when the sounds get too loud.

When I wake up one morning, I can hear music playing outside on the street. I get up from my bed and push aside the curtain to see where the music is coming from. The sunlight streams in, and I can see to the other side of the street. A man stands there turning a huge multicoloured wheel. First he uses one hand and then he uses the other hand. He puts his whole body behind turning the big wheel. It must be hard. It looks like he has to use all his strength. As he turns big wheel turns, the most wonderful sound comes out of the huge machine. Drums pounding and organ music make the most wonderful sounds to delight my ears. The organ music reminds me a little bit of the days when I was in the church, but this music is much happier. The organ is painted many different colours and it has pictures of animals on it. I can see dogs and cats and horses and bears painted on it, in many different colours. The man wears clothes that make him look funny. I go into the kitchen where Aunt Dora is making bread

"Auntie, do you hear the music outside?"

"Yes, Jackie that is the "orgel man" and the machine he plays his music on is called an "orgel." The orgel man (The organ grinder) has a monkey that collects money from the people that watch the show. Did you see his monkey?"

"No I did not see it." I am a little disappointed.

"Well, after breakfast you can go and watch the show and I am sure you will see the monkey too. You will enjoy it."

"Why are all these people here today?"

"It's called the kermis (carnival). They come once a year to entertain everybody and you can play games and watch a puppet show and have lots of fun." The whole sidewalk and the big empty spot behind it are taken up with brightly painted booths. People are standing and smiling while they eat the most wonderful delicacies.

After breakfast, Uncle Kees gives me a coin; he calls it a "Kwartje," and says; "go across the street and get anything you want for the money. This is the first time I have ever had my own money. When I walk to the other side of the street I am in a happy mood. Everybody is having fun. A large crowd stands in front of a puppet show. One of the puppets is beating the other one over the head with a stick while he screams really loud. Everybody watching is laughing; it is so funny. The grownups let all the little kids like me go all the way to the front so that we can see the show. I sit down on the grass and watch the show. The grass is a wet, but I don't care. Every other boy and girl is also sitting on the grass. Sitting there for a long time, I imagine myself in a big castle, like the puppets in the show, and I fight against the bad king who is very nasty to all the people. Then the show ends when the king is killed. Too bad that the show had to end. Further along is a man who puts a stick in his mouth while it is on fire. I am scared that he will burn his mouth. Then the tallest I have ever seen walks by me. His legs are so very long I have to look way up into the sun to see his head. There are so many things to see and do I don't know what to do first.

I walk by a man with a funny hat: "Hey kid do you want to win this big plush bear for a stuiver (five cents). He holds up a big bear. Sure, I want him for a stuiver.

"All you have to do, kid is throw one of your coins onto one of those plates over there." And he points at them with his stick. There are so many plates that I'm sure my coin will land on one of them. I can do that. So I throw my nickel at the plate. It lands on the plate and it rolls off the plate. "Oh, bad luck, come on kid try another stuiver, this time it'll stay on the plate." Yes, the man is right it was bad luck this time I'll win that big bear. I throw another nickel and my coin skips from one plate and lands on another and it slides off again. Now I don't need the man to tell me anymore to throw another coin. I throw another again and again and again.

"You got one more nickel. You'll win for sure this time."

Shaking my head, I squeeze the last coin in my hand. No way am I throwing this one.

"Ah, better luck next time, kid." says the man. "Now move on, kid. Other people want to play." Disappointed but much smarter I walk away. With my last stuiver I can still get me some candy.

"Aunt Dora with the money I'll get candy" I remember promising her.

I hand my last nickel to the candy lady, "What can I get for this?

"You can have some zoute drop, dubbel zout, and a candy cane and a piece of rock candy. Is that OK for you? She hands me the bag full of goodies. Happy with my treasure, I can go back without having to tell Auntie and Uncle that I lost almost all my money. This was definitely the most fun day I have ever had.

"Jackie did you know that today is a special day? It is the when we celebrate Queen Wilhemina birthday. So tonight, as a special treat and because you are such a good boy, we will drive to Amsterdam to watch the fireworks," Aunt Dora says. Excited, because I have never seen fireworks I can hardly wait to go.

"But first you have to eat something" She prepared a slice of bread and butter with hagelslag (Chocolate hail). Somehow I knew there would be a catch to this unexpected surprise. I can only eat a few bites.

"I'm not really hungry, Auntie," hoping that this won't spoil our trip to the city. She is in a good mood and says, "OK we'll put the rest of your sandwich in a little bag and you can eat it on the way"

Uncle Kees has a big shiny car. "This car is a 1946 Hudson Commodore Eight. I just picked it up from the dealer yesterday. You and Auntie are the first ones to get a ride in it. Isn't nice?" They let me sit in the front between them. I'm a little squeezed. Auntie is so fat. It's fine though, I have a great view.

Once we arrive in Amsterdam Uncle Kees looks for a place to park and we have to drive around and around. There are so many people with cars it's hard to find a parking space. He finds one on the Keizersgracht and we walk to where the fireworks will be let off, near het Damrak. There we wait until dark. Thousands of people are waiting around for the fireworks to start. Everybody seems so happy, laughing and singing and shouting. I can't see over the sea of heads so Uncle Kees puts me on his shoulders. Now it is dark enough for the fireworks to be set off. Kids are holding on to their Daddy's and Mommy's hands. Some are crying. Boy, this is so great. I have to look way up in the sky to see the fireworks change from sputtery white flames when they leave the ground into many coloured stars when they get high up into the night skies. They make huge booming noises. I don't know where to look first, there is so much fireworks all at once and the noise is deafening. I have to plug my ears with my hands. At the end a big sign lights up that says happy birthday to the Queen, uncle Kees tells me. It is over all too soon. Flushed with the excitement of the occasion I have to admit that this is the best firework I have ever seen. Come to think of it it's the only fireworks I have ever seen. I've had a wonderful day. How much better this day would have been if Mommy and Daddy could have seen this with me.

Aunt Dora and Uncle Kees are talking in the kitchen. They have a serious look on their faces. I've seen that look before. They are going to tell me something bad.

"Jackie" Uncle Kees says" We are going to Switzerland to pick up Maurice.

"That does not sound bad" I think. I am happy; I will get to see Maurice again.

Uncle Kees continues,"He has been staying in a Sanatorium in Switzerland for about one year now, he is feeling much better and it's about time that he comes home. While Auntie Dora and I go to pick him up, you will have to stay with another Aunt and Uncle."

I am very disappointed that I can't stay with them anymore, but I don't cry any longer. What's the point anyway?

"When are you going? I ask.

"We'll be leaving two days from now. First we will take you to Auntie Rosa and Uncle Levie in Amsterdam. You will really like them. They have a son and his name is Loekie."

CHAPTER 15

Auntie Roo, as she likes to be called and Uncle Levie live in an apartment with their son Loekie. Uncle Levie likes to make jokes. He always steals my nose. I laugh every time he does it, but I know that he is really holding his thumb between his two fingers, not my nose. He has no hair on his head. His head is shiny, and when he kisses you, his lips suck in your cheek. It feels so weird. He likes to whistle and sing. He sings a song about "Jansen who has a Jeep" and then he whistles the tune. The song makes me laugh. It is so funny. They like to go and visit people at night. Uncle Levie has a car. A red car. Uncle Levie says that it is a 1934 Ford sedan. I sit in the back all the time with Loukie. The seats are very hard and bouncy. They always stay too late when they visit and I get so sleepy. On the way home I fall asleep and Uncle Levie carries me upstairs to my bed. I get cranky once I am asleep and get woken up. My time is happy at Auntie Roo and Uncle Levie.

Loukie plays games with me. He has a hoop that he hits with a stick to make it move. He can really make it go fast. I try it a few times but I am not so good at it, because I can't run as fast as the hoop rolls. Loukie says, "Don't worry, once you're as old as me, you'll get better." He is nine years old and I'm five and a half. So all I can do for now is to watch him play. There is another game that other kids and he play together. It's called soccer. You play it with a big ball. The boys start out by picking teams, one boy at a time. I am always left to the last and nobody wants me. So I watch the boys play soccer. I really like to watch them play. They can kick the ball a mile. Sometimes the boys don't have a ball to play soccer with. So they roll up pieces of paper in a big ball and put rubber bands around it to keep it together.

They ask me, since I'm not playing, "Can we use you shoes to make a goal." I'm happy to give them my shoes, because now maybe they'll like me and they'll let me play with them next time.

Auntie Roo calls us in for supper. I want my shoes back. The boys are angry with me because I am taking their goal away. Loukie tells me to leave the shoes so I go home in bare feet.

Auntie Roo asks, "Where are your shoes?"

"I had to leave them; the boys needed them to make a goal."

"You go get them back right now. You can't be walking around without shoes. You'll get sick again and you'll have to go back to the hospital. She sends me back out to get my shoes.

The boys yell, "No! You can't have them; we're not finished with them. You'll have to wait," I tell them I'll get Loukie. The boys give me my shoes right away. Loukie is big for his age.

The day comes when they tell me that they don't want me anymore. "It's not that we don't want you to live with us. But you see, we are going to live in Canada soon and you don't have any papers and that is why you can't go with us." We will take you to live with your Auntie Judith and Uncle Jopie Dinsdag.

I wish Mommy and Daddy were here.

The next morning my little suitcase packed with all my belongings is loaded into the 1934 Ford Sedan and we go to the house of Jopie and Judith Dinsdag. After a short drive across the city we get to their house. I look at Judith and I think that she is the most beautiful lady I have ever seen. She has black hair and red lips. Her nails are long and they are painted red too. I sniff the smell around her and it smells really good. The dress she wears is also red She bends down and gives me a hug and a kiss on the cheek. Jopie her husband has a crooked mouth when he talks. He always has a cigar in his mouth and he keeps lighting matches to keep it burning. He chews on the cigar and the end is wet and dirty. I try not to look at his crooked mouth but my eyes always go there. When I look at my face in the hall mirror, and when nobody is watching me, I make my mouth in the same shape as Jopie's to see how it looks on me. It looks funny and it makes me laugh. Jopie's mouth is brown from the cigar. I don't like his mouth, it stinks. When he talks spit comes out. I try not to be where he talks. Judith and Jopie have no children of their own.

"You want to eat something boy? Asks Uncle Jopie.

"No sir I'm not hungry."

"Well, you'll have to eat something; you want to grow up to be big and strong. You want to be big and strong, don't you, boy?

"My name is Jackie, sir."

"Ok, boy we'll let it go for now, but starting tomorrow we'll start fattening you up. You must be tired so maybe we'll get you ready for bed. You'll have an appetite in the morning."

"Yes sir."

CHAPTER 16

The following morning I can't stay in bed any longer. I get up and tiptoe to the bathroom to have a peepee. Judith is brushing her hair.

"Jackie, where is your toothbrush?"

"I don't have a toothbrush."

"How do you brush your teeth if you don't have a toothbrush?

"I don't brush my teeth Auntie."

"You have to brush your teeth every day, otherwise they will all fall out of your mouth. You don't want your teeth to fall out do you?"

"No Auntie." Now I am really scared my teeth will fall out and I touch them to see if any are loose. They feel pretty tight.

"Well, we'll have to go to the store and buy you a toothbrush. Would you like that?'

"Yes Auntie."

Walking down the street from where she lives we suddenly hear someone screaming and we both look around to see where the screaming is coming from. Behind us a man is pulling a woman by the hair. She stumbles and falls to the ground. The man does not stop but keeps pulling her by the hair. He is dragging her along the ground now. She is holding on to her hair and she is screaming in pain. She has a card around her neck. Judith says that on it is written: "Vuile Hoer" (Dirty Whore). Judith says that the woman had gone to bed with a German soldier and now she is pregnant with his child. Her husband just came back from the war and found out. Judith says the woman is getting what she deserves. By now, the man is kicking her in the stomach many times. The woman screams and is lying on the ground in a ball trying to protect her stomach.

All the time the man is yelling at his wife, "Vuile Hoer, Vuile hoer." I am so upset. I want to scream at him to stop hurting her. A crowd has gathered and is watching in silence. Nobody is lifting a finger to help the woman. My heart is crying. "Stop it, stop it." I keep yelling inside my head. Finally, the man is tired of kicking his wife and leaves her on the sidewalk while he walks back to his house. He screams at her that she cannot come back to his house anymore. She lies there crying and everybody walks away.

"Is nobody going to help her?" I ask Judith.

"No, absolutely not, he should have killed her." She replies.

"Why did the man kick her so much, Auntie? Didn't he know he was hurting her?" I can't possibly understand it. I feel very bad for the woman. I want to go over to the woman and tell her that everything is going to be OK. Judith drags me away from this terrible scene. We go inside the house. I don't want to tell Judith she did not get me a toothbrush for my teeth. She tells Jopie the story and he keeps on saying "Vuile Hoer, he should have killed her as well as the dirty kraut baby."

At this point I can't help myself anymore and I scream "Why is everybody so terribly mean?" "Maybe the woman made a mistake, but the baby can't help it. Why should the baby be killed?"

"You're just a child; you don't know what's going on."

I keep quiet now, because otherwise he might send me away. The whole day and the next I am terribly upset at what I saw.

After a few days, they sit me down and they tell me that they cannot look after Maurice and me. Where is Maurice? I have not seen him for such a long time. I miss him so very much. Judith and Jopie keep talking to me but I don't hear what they are saying. I nod every so often. In the end they tell me that Uncle Jules is coming to pick me up the following day and that I will be flying home with him, in an airplane. I can't believe my ears. Me in an airplane? I have never been in one. I can't wait till tomorrow. When it is time to go to bed, I am not sleepy. I lay with my eyes open in the dark bedroom waiting for tomorrow to come.

CHAPTER 17

I n the morning, a car pulls up in front of Judith and Jopie Dinsdag house and Uncle Jules comes out of the car. Running towards him I tell him that I am happy to see him; maybe he likes to hear that. He pats me on the head.

"Where is his suitcase, Jopie?"

"It's in the house I'll get it"

Judith gives me a hug and Jopie puts the suitcase in the trunk of the car. He bends down to give me a kiss on the cheek and I hold my breath as long as I can, until he is gone from my face.

I get in the backseat of the big black car and Uncle Jules sits down beside me.

"Who is driving the car Uncle Jules?"

"This is a limousine and it comes with a chauffeur. The chauffeur will drive the car to the airport, Schiphol." I sit back and I enjoy the long ride." We arrive at the airport. A man in a red cap takes our suitcases. We go inside a building where many people are moving, here and there. Some are standing at counters talking to pretty ladies with hats on. All the ladies wear the same clothes. I have never seen so many beautiful ladies in one place before. It's our turn to talk to one of the pretty ladies. Uncle Jules says hello. The lady answers by saying." May I see your tickets please?" Uncle Jules then hands her some papers. I hope he knows what a ticket is because I don't know. Just outside the door, on the other side of the counter, there are many planes. I have never seen planes on the ground before. They have always been in the air. The lady hands Uncle Jules back the paper and wishes him a good trip. She does not wish me a good trip. A loud voice comes out of nowhere and says that the plane to Melsbroek is ready to board "That's us," says

Uncle Jules. He takes me by the hand and we walk onto the tarmac towards the plane. We climb the ladder that stands in front of the door of the plane. The steps are too high for me to climb by myself. Uncle Jules picks me up and carries me up the stairs. Once inside the plane, another very pretty lady takes our tickets and shows us where we have to sit. She gives Uncle Jules and me a piece of chewing gum. She carefully explains to us that once the plane starts we have to put the chewing gum in our mouths and chew hard on it with our mouths open, otherwise, our ears will pop. When the plane takes off, I chew on that gum as if my life depended on it. I don't want to have popped ears.

Looking out the aircraft window I see the ground disappear. The houses below become smaller and smaller and suddenly we are in the clouds. What a wonderful sight it is. The one thing that really bothers me is the loud sound of the engines. It is deafening. I put my hands over my ears but it does not help because the sound seems to be inside my body. After a while, I kind of get used to it and it does not bother me as much. A stewardess comes around and offers everyone something to drink.

"Have a Coca Cola says," Uncle Jules says. I've never had Coca Cola before. It tastes sweet and very fizzy. When I pour the Coca Cola in the cup the fizz jumps up and when I drink, some of the fizz hits my nose. "Drink it nice and slow a few sips at the time." I drink and it makes me hiccup. I guess I drank too fast, so now I take small little sips and I don't hiccup. But I have to burp. A very loud burp comes out. It is so loud my face turns red. Uncle Jules laughs.

A voice announces that we will be landing at Melsbroek and that we need to fasten our seatbelts. Mine is already fastened, from before, so I relax. I can feel the plane turn first to one side and then the other. As it hits the ground, the plane makes me jump up from my seat. That scares me. Uncle Jules is smiling so I guess everything is fine. Now we get into another car and we have to go for a very long drive. After what seems forever, we arrive at a house. Uncle Jules explains that this is where he and Aunt Ninon live with Raymond and Juliana.

"From now on this will be your new house too. You and your brother Maurice will be living with Aunt Ninon and me and our two children. You remember them, don't you?" I don't remember.

CHAPTER 18.
Jackie's War

I don't want to call you Mommy and Daddy, I already have a Mommy and Daddy," I answer, "and they are coming to get me when they come back from Switzerland. They promised. Maurice said they will be back soon," Aunt Ninon and Uncle Jules have sad looks on their faces and aunt Ninon starts to cry." Why does she cry? She should be happy instead. I just told her my Mommy and Daddy are coming.

***

The Big Three Allied leaders, Stalin, Churchill and Roosevelt, came together in a secret conference at Yalta held in the Crimea on February 4-11, 1945. At this conference, Stalin, Churchill, and Roosevelt talked about the reorganization of Europe. The main purpose is to re-establish the nations that have been captured and destroyed by Germany.

Dividing the occupied Germany is one of their top priorities. Stalin, Churchill and Roosevelt agree to divide Germany into three zones giving control to the three nations present. Because of the immense size of Stalin's army, Russia takes Berlin and control of the eastern half of Germany. Great Britain suggests that France should also be one of the occupiers. Stalin disagrees but he eventually agrees. Poland becomes independent once more and holds its own national elections to create a new, independent government. Yugoslavia is also allowed its own government, which consists of mostly members of the old government. Neither Poland nor Yugoslavia is allowed to have Nazi or Fascist leaders in their new governments.

Stalin promises to fight Japan and in return expects to occupy areas in the East. Roosevelt, Churchill, and Stalin ratified the secret Yalta agreement on February 11, 1945. The United States, Britain and Russia gave themselves complete authority to do anything necessary to prevent future German aggression, including the dismemberment of Germany.

*****

Aunt Ninon is worried about me. "Jackie you have to eat to build up your strength. You are still very weak from when you were sick with pleurisy and pneumonia and you were burned too, with boiling milk. You were in many different hospitals in Holland and here in Belgium. Remember? And you did not have enough food to eat. Remember?"

I do remember.

I get the measles and the chicken pox one after the other. Chicken pox is worse because than the measles because it itches.

Auntie says "Don't scratch, it will leave marks on your body." I can't help scratching myself, when nobody is looking.

I cough all the time.

Aunt Ninon asks me "are you coughing?"

"No I'm OK. I just have an itch in my throat." She worries too much about me.

"Everybody has to have a poop in the morning, first thing after you get up," Auntie says.

"I don't have to poop first thing in the morning.   " You must try, it's good for you. You can't leave the toilet until after you've pooped."

So, every morning, after getting up, I have to sit on the toilet to have a poop. I sit for so long that my one leg goes to sleep. After pushing and pushing, till I am blue in the face, a little bit of poop comes out. Aunt Ninon checks to see that it's enough and if she says, "yes", I am allowed off the toilet. I try standing on my one leg that went to sleep and I almost fall over. It feels funny and thick; I can't walk on it right away. After a time the feeling returns in my leg and I can put my weight on it. Every morning we go through the same thing.

"I know what your problem is," she says, "You can't poop because you are constipated. I will give you an enema."

She puts a rubber tube up my butt. At he end of the tube, the part she holds in her hand, is a large black ball which she starts to squeeze. I can feel some warm stuff going into my behind. Juliana is watching me. Raymond is giggling. He thinks it's funny. This is so embarrassing. I stand there, in the middle of the kitchen, with no clothes on, with a tube coming out of my ass. By now Raymond is rolling around the floor killing himself with laughter. Before long I feel things starting to rumble in my tummy.

"I got to go," I scream.

"Hold on, not so fast" she says."

"I'll shit on the floor" I tell her with mounting panic.

"Hold it just a while longer, you are almost ready."

"I can't hold it any longer." I run to the toilet. The tube comes out and Auntie is still holding on to the ball. "Wait" she screams. At this point I don't care whether she wants me to hold it one more second or a half an hour. I just make it to the toilet in time. I sit down and I let go. What a relief. The poop comes out like water. And it sounds like one long fart that does not stop. Boy, it feels so good. Raymond now stands beside me in the bathroom and pats me on the shoulder. "You did good," he says with admiration in his voice, "I thought for sure you would shit on the kitchen floor. That would have been a mess."

Auntie gives him a whack on the back of the head; "Don't use that word, say kaka."

"Jackie said it first." Raymond rubs his sore head.

"He doesn't know any better and you do."

I think to myself that's gotta be a month's worth, at least. I don't ever want to have another enema. Having nothing left to poop out the following few days causes Auntie a lot of worry. Doesn't she realize I got rid of everything the day of the enema?

I am outside, by myself on the deserted street. I now live at seven Hercules Straat in Berchem, near Antwerp. Aunt Ninon tells me I have to remember where we live.

She asks me everyday;" Jackie where do we live"

"7 Hercules Straat in Berchem," I answer with pride. I don't really know why she keeps asking me. I wish she could remember it on her own by now.

Everywhere I look, buildings are in pieces. Red bricks are scattered all over the place. Piles of rubble line the streets, where houses once stood. There are no trees or grass anywhere. Maurice calls these places, ruins. Nobody lives in them. Did people live there before? Where are they now? I wonder. The sun is bright in the sky. I want to look away, but I keep looking into the sun. After a long time I lower my eyes and I see black spots. I do it again and again. I am tired of this game now and anyways I don't feel so good.

Maurice comes out of the house. Aunt Ninon has been yelling at him. He peed in his bed again and she wrapped him in the wet sheets and shoved him out on the street so that everyone could see what he had done. I hate her for doing that to my brother. I pee in my bed every night and she never wraps me in the bed sheets. He wants to play a game.

"You'll be the Kraut and I'll be the Canadian soldier," he says "and I'll shoot you."

"I want to be the Canadian soldier this time and you be the Kraut" I complain.

"You have to know how to be a Canadian soldier and you've never been one so that's why you can't be one."

"I know Marty and Earl, they are Canadian soldiers." I say with not much conviction. So I play the Kraut again. We play in the broken buildings. Aunt Ninon has told us never to play in the bombed buildings, they are far too dangerous to play in, but we go there anyways, we do not see any bombs.

"Maurice, Aunt Ninon will yell at us when she finds out that we've played in the ruins again"

"You tell her and I'll kill you" he threatens.

"I won't tell."

"Jackie, Maurice, supper." A feeling of panic overtakes me and my stomach is starting to feel funny again.

CHAPTER 19

Aunt Ninon is scooping generous amounts of food on everyone's plate.

"Please, not so much for me. I'm not hungry." I complain. She ignores me and for good measure scoops even more on my plate, it seems. My panic increases and I can feel a wave of nausea coming from the depths of my stomach. The plate of food in front of me is so big. There is no way that I can eat all the food on my plate. I feel like crying. I want to tell her she gave me too much food, but then she'll be angry with me again, and I hate that. I don't like anyone yelling at me. I want everyone to like me.

"Eat every last morsel from your plate, before you leave the table. Millions of children in the world go hungry every day," Auntie insists. Hours later, alone and feeling completely miserable I am allowed to get up from the table, not having eaten one bit of food from my plate. I don't feel good about it and Auntie says that I am a waster of good food. And so it goes at every meal, until at one point Aunt Ninon gets angry and frustrated. She takes the food that I just vomited up, scoops it up, shoves it into my mouth and says; "Swallow it!" I swallow and the food comes right back up, all over the table cloth.

"You go to bed without supper and you stay there until you are ready to eat," she screams.

I stay in bed for three days not feeling the least bit hungry.

Aunt Ninon takes me to see a doctor.

"The kid is severely malnourished," he tells her. "It will take some time before he'll be able to retain food. I'll prescribe some cod liver oil which he must take twice daily, and I'll also prescribe some vitamins. The cod liver oil tastes awful, but I manage to keep it down. I feel very guilty for not being able to eat and everybody makes fun of me.

"Jackie is a baby, he can't eat by himself," Raymond sings the words. If I was only bigger I'd slap him for making me feel so bad.

Aunt Ninon says to Juliana: "Since Jackie can't eat on his own you feed him." I sit there, humiliated, while Juliana scoops food into my mouth. Maurice never makes fun of me. He tells me everything is going to be fine. "As soon as Mommy and Daddy come to get us, you'll be OK again. You'll be eating lots of food then and you won't feel sick to your stomach anymore, you'll see." So, I wait with hope for the day to arrive when Mommy and Daddy will come and rescue us. Days turn into months but they don't come.

"Maybe they don't know that we are here." I tell Maurice

"Do you think so?" I am disappointed by his question. I wanted him to tell me that he is sure they will show up.

Raymond is mean to Maurice; he gets him into trouble all the time. He'll break something on purpose and says that Maurice broke it. Maurice is punished and beaten and Raymond laughs when that happens. I hate Raymond. Juliana and I get along fine. Every Sunday, if the children have been good all week, we are allowed to go to the movies. This is the best time of the entire week. We can't wait for Sunday to arrive. In the morning we get bathed and then we all put on our Sunday best clothes. In the afternoon, we go to the movies. In Berchem, there are three movie theaters. The Luxor, the Cineac, the Paramount. I like adventure movies with Errol Flynn, Gary Cooper and John Wayne. I also like Westerns and Musicals, or comedies with Charlie Chaplin, The Marx Brothers the Ritz Brothers and the Three Stooges. I don't like movies with a lot of kissing in them. Most often we all get to go but sometimes, when Maurice has done something bad, Aunt Ninon tells him that for his punishment he can't go to the movies. When we leave the house we all walk together hand in hand. Raymond is the one that looks after everybody because he is the oldest. He is also the one that carries the money to pay for the movie. Aunt Ninon gives us a bag of candies so that we can eat them while we are in the movie theater.

As much as I want to remember Mommy and Daddy, I have trouble remembering what they look like. We stop playing and then Maurice and I talk about them and he says that everything will be fine again once they come to get us back. Maurice says that he misses them more than me because he is older than I am. And he remembers their faces.

"Do you remember Mommy and daddy's faces?" he asks. I remember my Mommy's hugs and how she used to hold me so close and that is what I miss the most. Daddy did not hug me like that. He would pat me on the head and he would tell me that I was a good boy. And then we start to play again.

I am six years old now and Maurice is ten and a half, he says.

Uncle Jules is always working. "Away on business," he says. Aunt Ninon is never away on business so we get to stay with her all the time. She tells us that if we are bad she will tell Uncle Jules. That's scary. When she tells him that we were bad and tired her out, he usually gives us a slap on the head or on the bottom. It hurts. So we try to be good all the times. Sometimes though, I can't help it if a plate falls down and breaks or I spill my milk on the clean white tablecloth. Raymond always wants to get us into trouble, especially Maurice.

CHAPTER 20

Uncle Jules and aunt Ninon are sitting at the table with Maurice and me. They talk about the war and about being Jewish.

"We are Jewish," he says, "and that is why this war was so bad for us. The dirty Krauts would pick on us poor Jews and whenever they found one of us, they would put us in cattle cars and take us to concentration camps, where they would do very bad things to us. You must hate the Germans for what they did. Most of the Jews that went to the concentration camps never came back from there. Your Mommy and Daddy, tried to get away from the Germans by escaping to Switzerland."

"Why didn't they take us with them?" asks Maurice.

"Because they felt that you had a better chance by staying in Holland. Neither you nor Jackie look Jewish, you both have blond hair and blue eyes, so nobody could tell you were Jewish. That is why they left you with the neighbours."

"When are they coming to get us?" I ask.

"They are not coming to get you."

"Why not, don't they love us anymore?"

"It's not that. They were taken by the Gestapo and sent to a concentration camp, they had to work very hard in the concentration camp and they hardly got anything to eat, so they got sick and eventually they died in the concentration camp. We are very sorry to have to tell you this"

"No, they are coming to get us, Maurice promised me. I feel for his hand and I hold on to it. He is the only brother I have.

"I'll look after you Jackie," he whispers in my ear. I believe him.

"We promised your Mommy and Daddy that if anything happened to them that we would take care of Maurice and you and that we will be your father and mother from now on.

"You can't be our Mommy and Daddy. We already have a Mommy and Daddy. Why did they leave us? They should have taken us with them. Why?" I am angry now. "They should have asked us to come with them Maurice." I look at his face and he nods. And now Mommy and Daddy are not coming back. Aunt and Uncle can't take care of us. It's not the same. Only Mommy and Daddy can do that job. Not aunts and uncles. Why not? Because we don't belong to Aunts and Uncles. We belong to Mommy and Daddy. They have to look after us. Aunts and uncles don't have to look after us. I can't understand why Aunt Ninon and Uncle Jules would want to look after us. I don't understand.

"What is going to happen to us Maurice? I'm scared. There is no Mommy and Daddy to belong to."

"You belong to me. We belong together forever," He says in a soft voice.

CHAPTER 21

Aunt Ninon complains that things are hard to come by; she says that everything is rationed. We are lucky in a way because Uncle Jules sells fruit to stores so we have all the fresh fruit we want and a few vegetables, no meat, few eggs, no soap, and no toilet paper. It is difficult for everybody and we have to stand in line for hours for some of the things we need.

"If you have enough money you can buy everything needed on the black market. But most people don't have any money so they have to do without." says Auntie. I think people in the black market are bad people because if you don't have any money they won't give you anything even if you really need it.

One day, a boy I've never seen before, comes up to me and says, "You are a dirty Jew." I am scared. I don't know what to do. How does he know I am a Jew? I'm not dirty. I don't even know him. When I get home, I tell them that some boy called me a dirty Jew. Uncle Jules is very upset and asks me what I did about it.

"Nothing, I did not know what to do," I said.

"You got to beat him up to defend the Jews and the memory of your parents." Uncle Jules says in a loud voice, "you will find in life that everybody hates the Jews, thanks to Hitler and the Germans. You've got to hate all the Germans for what they did to us Jews."

Hate is a new word. How does hate me you feel? What does it mean? Does it mean you're not supposed to like them? Or is it worse than that?

"Hate is the feeling you have when somebody does something very bad to you and you have to be bad right back to them," Maurice says "and if you have a gun, you have to shoot them. If you have no gun, you have to hit them with your fists. If you can't do it yourself because you're too small, just come and get me and I will beat them up for you."

With that explanation, I feel much better because now I know what to do when I hate somebody.

The next day the same boy calls me a dirty Jew again and now I hate him. As I want to hit him, he runs away. I try to catch him but he is way too fast.

From a safe distance he yells at me,"dirty Jew, dirty Jew" over and over. Passersby look at me in a strange way and I feel ashamed. I want to run away and tell them that it's not me the boy is yelling at, but somebody else. I walk home and now I hate the boy so much that I am thinking of the terrible things I will do to him if I ever catch him. I can't run as fast as the boy and no matter how hard I try I can't catch him, until one day as he walks by our house I just come out and there he is. I grab him as he tries to run away. I am ready to hit him and he starts to cry,"I am sorry I called you a dirty Jew. I won't do it anymore." I let him go and he runs and then stops. From a safe distance he starts to yell,"dirty Jew, dirty Jew." Angry and ashamed, but much smarter now I decide never to believe anything anyone tells me again.

CHAPTER 22

I still have trouble eating and I still get sick to my stomach as I swallow food.

"Jackie needs an operation to have his tonsils removed. The boy has trouble swallowing because his tonsils are so large they cause him to become nauseous when he swallows," the doctor says.

On the day of the operation Auntie says, "Raymond since you are the oldest you have to look after the others while I take Jackie to the hospitals to have his tonsils removed. Can you do that without getting into any trouble?"

"Yes Mommy. Don't worry." He has a twinkle in his eye and I feel somehow that he will be dreaming up a plan to torment Maurice. "Why does Auntie not see this I wonder?" Once at the hospital I have to take off my clothes and put on a hospital gown that the nurse hands me.

"Take off all your clothes including your underwear. Put the gown on with the open side towards the back," she instructs me in a pleasant voice. She takes me by the hand to the operating room, while I try to keep the back of my gown closed with my free hand. I don't want anyone to see my bare bum. "Sit down in the chair," the doctor commands. The chair looks a little like a bed with the head part up and the part where my legs go is down. It's quite comfortable. "Are you nervous," the doctor asks

"No sir."

He puts a mask over my mouth "Breath in really deep. Can you do that?" he asks. All I can do is nod.

I hear someone calling my name,"Jackie, Jackie you can wake up now. The operation is over." I open my eyes and I am lying in a hospital bed. When I try to Swallowing is really difficult. My throat really hurts. The nurse gives me some ice to suck on. Aunt Ninon is sitting in the room. She smiles," We can go home soon and because you've been such a good boy I will give you ice cream to eat. It'll be really good for your throat and it won't hurt so bad to swallow." She is wrong; my throat hurts very badly when I eat ice cream. I can hardly swallow. After a few days, though, my throat hurts less and less. The doctor was right, when he said, "Jackie will get his appetite back with his tonsils removed." When I swallow my food now I don't feel sick anymore. Actually, I always feel hungry now and I look forward to eating.

"It is time for you to start school young man," Auntie says one day. Maurice, Raymond and I will go to the same school so on one bright sunny morning we all leave home together. I hold on to Maurice's hand, afraid to let go, ready for a grand new adventure. SOJ 1 is the school we go to. It is on 17 Louisa Street in Antwerp. We get on one streetcar first, and after three stops, we have to get on a different streetcar for eight stops. Then we have to walk for a while and finally we arrive at the school. The first day of school is very exciting. We are all told where to line up. We have to line up in front of our teacher, in rows of two by two. I am in class 1A Mr. Williamson is my teacher. He has a list from which he reads off all the names of the kids in the class. He calls my name off as Jack Veefer. "It's not Veefer, sir," I protest,"its Veffer." There are many boys in the class, but no girls. Mr. Williamson tells us, "Repeat after me boys" and he starts says, "One" and everyone repeats the numbers he says "1, 2, 3, 4, 5, 6, 7, 8, 9, 10." This is fun. I really like school. After the counting, he gives everyone a page with a picture on it," Use you colour crayons I gave you to paint in the colours on the picture. Now, make sure you colour inside the lines. The boy that has the best coloured picture will get a prize," and he holds up a sucker. As hard as I try to stay inside the lines my pencil always goes outside of the lines. I did not win. I feel bad because I really wanted that sucker. At lunch time a bell rings very loud and it scares me half to death. Mr. Williamson tells us, "It's time to eat your lunch now. Put your pencils and paper aside and eat your lunch. You have one hour for lunch." Each of us brought a bag with a sandwich in it. My sandwich has butter and cheese on it. Auntie also put a bottle of milk, and an apple in my lunch bag. After we finish eating lunch, we are allowed to play in the schoolyard. School is fun. I learn a lot of stuff I didn't know before.

I have a friend at school. His name is Freddie de Koch. We met on the first day of school and we like each other right away. He never makes fun of me or calls me names. I can share anything with him even my deepest secrets. I have never had a friend before. We sit next to each other in class. It is so wonderful to have a best friend. Maurice is in grade three and so is Raymond. They are in the same class.

Aunt Ninon says to us all"It's time for you kids to learn how to swim. It's an important life skill, so we have enrolled you every Wednesday evening from six to seven to take swimming lessons." After we get home from school we get our bathing suits and towels and we have to take the streetcar again to go to the Astrid Bad in the Nervier Street in Antwerp. So Raymond, Maurice, Juliana and I all go to the swim club. Mr. Maurice Blitz, our swimming instructor, is a nice man. His tummy is very big. Somebody says that he was a champion swimmer when he was younger. He teaches us to thread water by moving our arms and hands and legs. We have to do this for many weeks. We keep asking," When can we swim?" We all get so bored. Mr. Blitz likes Juliana. He swims on his back and then he puts her on his fat belly. It looks like Juliana is floating around on an island.

One day Mr. Blitz announces,"You have all mastered the art of staying afloat. None of you have drowned, so now let's see if I can teach you how to swim." He gives each of us a wooden board and he tells us to hold on to it with our hands and start to move our legs like frogs do. At first, my legs won't stay up. They keep sinking down. After a while, though, I can keep them up and I'm actually moving forward in the water. So is Juliana, she keeps right up with me.

After several weeks of doing the same, Mr. Blitz says that we are now ready to use both our arms and our legs to swim. He stands at the edge of the water and holds out a long pole in front of me and tells me I have to swim and if I get tired to hold on to the pole. I start out fine but when I get near the deep end I get scared, I feel myself sinking, and I grab the pole. Mr. Blitz says, "Don't do that. You are just scared. Jackie, you can swim" That easy for him to say, but if I can swim why do I keep sinking? At last, after many tries I manage to stay up for most of the length of the pool. As time passes, I can now swim several lengths of the pool. We are all very proud of ourselves.

Mr. Blitz blows his whistle,"everyone out of the pool. The lesson is over for tonight." The water is very cold and Mr. Blitz tells us we had better go under the hot showers to warm up. I am in a shower by myself, actually, the water is quite cold and I am shivering. A man comes into the stall and says that he can warm me up. He rubs his crotch into me. He says "Put your hand inside my bathing suit it'll warm you up." I get so scared I run away from him. I don't tell anyone because I figure I'll get into trouble if I do.

After we get home from swimming Aunt Ninon always has warm soup and buttered bread ready for us to eat. I can't stop eating, I am so hungry. Mr. Blitz is very happy with my progress and he tells me that next week there is a swim meet and the club will be competing against other swim clubs. He thinks I am good enough to compete in the 50-meter breaststroke event. I am excited about the idea. I have never competed in anything. If Mr. Blitz thinks that I am good enough to win that makes me very proud. I can't wait to get home so that I can tell Aunt and Uncle the good news. I am proud of myself and I start to tell them about how I have been chosen to represent the swim club in the 50-meter breaststroke and Mr. Blitz says that I can actually win the event for the club. Aunt Ninon bursts my bubble "There will be no competing for you. You are much too weak, you have been sick with pneumonia and pleurisy and when you exert yourself in a competition like that you will get sick again." I am utterly shattered. I start to cry,"Auntie it's not fair I feel fine. I won't get sick I promise.

"If you don't stop crying, I'll give you a spanking and then you'll have something to cry about." Dejected and feeling terribly alone I go sit in the front room with my only book, my primary reading book, and lose myself in the wonderful short stories.

CHAPTER 23

There is an organization that we belong to. It's for boys as well as girls. Kindervreugd, is its name. If you can't afford to pay Kindervreugd sends kids to the Seashore. This summer Maurice and I are chosen to go on a vacation to Blankenberge, a seaside resort on the North Sea. We are allowed to stay for the whole two months' summer holiday. We don't know anyone when we arrive. We stick close together. The first few days are strange and lonely. Once we're used to it and we make friends with the other kids we feel very comfortable. We're having an absolutely wonderful time. We all eat together in this huge dining room. The athletic director, Mr. Pons, was in the war. He was put in prison and the Germans tortured him. He got put on a rack and they stretched him. It made me sick when one of my new friends at camp first told us. He says,"it was horrible. They tied him on this rack and the krauts started to pull his arms at one end and some others pulled his legs at the other end. And he screamed a lot. It hurt. Wouldn't you scream?" We can see the stretch marks behind his knees and his armpits where the skin tore open as he was being tortured. We didn't bother asking the boy how come he knew so much about the torturing. Maybe he was there I suppose. Mr. Pons is very nice to Maurice and me. He leads all the kids in exercises every day. We get to eat our meals in a very big dining hall. There must be hundreds of kids from all different places. I am so hungry all the time now. In the morning they let us have eggs and toast and orange juice. No coffee though. They say we are too young for coffee. But Auntie gives me coffee every morning. I get to drink milk instead. For lunch we usually have potatoes and vegetables and meat. I don't know what kind of meat it is most of the time. Maurice likes the food too. We sleep in the same room in bunk beds. He uses the bed on top and I sleep in the bottom bunk. "You'll fall out of the top bunk on your head," he says. I don't want to fall on my head, so I feel lucky I can sleep in the lower bunk. Mr. Pons arranges games on the beach. When we don't play games we like to build sand castles and we go swimming in the sea. I get badly sunburned on the first day, though. It's really sore, especially on my chest. The two months fly by and our vacation comes to an end far too soon. All the kids board busses and head back home. Mr. Pons stands with a clipboard in his hand telling everyone what bus to get on. Maurice and I have to get into the bus with the number 13 on it. It goes all the way to Antwerp. "Kids don't get on the wrong bus," he cautions,"you don't want to wind up in the wrong place. Good bye kids, it's been fun. We'll see you this time next year." he adds with a smile. And then he waves at us when the busses drive away. I think he gave me a special little wave and a wink of an eye. Gee, how I love Mr. Pons. I'll always remember him. I make a promise to myself that I will be coming back here for my next summer vacation.

We were kept so busy that we did not think about Mommy and Daddy once during the whole time.

My friend and companion at home, besides my brother Maurice, is Juliana. Though she is a year or so younger, we get along well. We play games together and when Maurice and I go for walks, she wants to tag along. The only thing I don't like about her is that if Maurice and I do something bad she tells and then we get into trouble, mostly we'll get yelled at and often we'll get a spanking from uncle Jules. Aunt Ninon always tells us that she will tell uncle Jules when we've done something bad and she usually does. The way she does it is by putting on a "nebbish" face when he gets home. With a worried look he asks her;" what's wrong?" At first she says:"Oh, nothing". Then with some more prompting, she'll make up a story of how bad we've been. I feel like saying to Uncle, "she's lying. I did not break that plate on purpose. It fell out of my hand after Juliana pushed me. I couldn't help it that the food got all over the floor and she slipped on it and fell when she tried to run after me to give me a slap. Honest."

By the time she is finished, Uncle Jules is steaming mad and gives us a spanking. I hate it when she does that.

Uncle Jules is Jewish and aunt Ninon is Catholic. I am curious about certain things. Religion is a taboo subject in the house. So I dare not ask questions. Uncle Jules says,

"If God was such a loving God, why did He let six million Jews die in the concentration camps? Being Jewish has always been a burden throughout our Jewish history," he says. "Better to be nothing." Aunt Ninon says that being a Catholic is not much better, because there are too many rules and regulations and the rules don't make any sense. She says God is Jesus Christ. I have the feeling deep inside that there is only one God and he is the same God for Jews and for Catholics. I have felt this way ever since I was in the church with Marain and Parain on Sundays. It felt a wonderful happiness in the church. I can feel it but I can't explain it. Then the feeling leaves when the pastor starts to talk. He chases it all away in a moment. I feel that God wants us to be happy and not sad and we have to like each other a lot. The pastor tells these long stories. Everybody is so serious when they listen to him. He makes me want to go to sleep. I am not so sure that the pastor tells us what God wants us to know. I promise myself that when I am old enough I'll try to figure it out for myself.

CHAPTER 24

St. Nicholas comes on December 6. He arrives riding on a white horse with his black servant in tow. His servant's name is "Zwarte Piet." All the children have to be extra good at that time; otherwise, St. Nicholas will not bring any presents to the children. With great anticipation, we await his arrival on the night of December 6. We go to bed early and get up extra early the next morning to see if St. Nick brought toys and treats. There in its entire shining splendour, he left me a colt 45 in a leather holster and a book entitled Pietje Bell. He also left me some oranges and chocolates. I am thrilled. This is my very own first book. Now I finally have something new I can read besides my first grade reader. I strap on the gun and walk around with it all day. It shoots caps and it makes a loud noise. Auntie says, "Stop shooting your gun in the house." I sit and start to read my book, and suddenly, I am transported into a wonderful new world of imagination. Pietje Bell likes to play tricks. He makes me laugh so hard that I can't stop. Oh, how I love to read. I forget about everything else when I read. When people call me, I don't hear them, once I am involved in my book. Aunt Ninon gets mad at me; she thinks I do it on purpose. She says,"put away that book. You are not allowed to read anymore until you learn to listen."

"I listen Auntie; I can't help it if I don't hear you. I'm sorry it won't happen again." She will not let me read my book for the rest of the day. I want to play with my gun, and then I remember I can't shoot it in the house. There is not very much I can do. So Maurice and I go outside to play. It's very cold and we have nothing to do with so we play war again. He is the Canadian soldier, I am the Kraut, and we play in the ruins. He chases me with a long stick that's his rifle. I have my cap gun and I keep shooting at him but he won't fall down dead. I say, "Maurice you're dead" Maurice says, "You can't kill a Canadian soldier. So he keeps chasing me until he says he's killed me. "You can kill German soldiers," he says.

We don't care if Aunt Ninon finds out that we've played in the ruins.

On December 31st. I read a New Years greeting to Aunt and Uncle. This message has been carefully prepared by the teacher and meticulously copied by each student to be read aloud to parents on New Years Eve. The message starts out "Dearest Mommy and Daddy." When I read the words, I feel weird, knowing that aunt and uncle are not my mommy and daddy. The message continues to speak in lofty terms about mommy and daddy. At the end of it, I realize these words are not meant for them but for my real Mommy and Daddy. I get touched by the moment and I can't help crying, eventhough I don't want to. Aunt and Uncle think I cry for them and they are touched. They both hug me.

CHAPTER 25

It is summer 1947. School is out for the summer. Uncle Jules says that we are all going to go to the seashore. He has rented a house for the next two months. The following morning we pack our things and pack them into Uncle's truck. Uncle has no regular car. Aunt Ninon, Uncle Jules and Juliana sit together in the front cab. Maurice, Raymond and I have to sit in the back of the truck. There is no light in the back. Once the door is closed it is pitch black. At first, it scares me to sit in complete darkness. After a while, though, my eyes get used to the darkness and we play word games. We can't move around too much because when we do we trip over the boxes and the luggage. We have to hold on tight, the road is bumpy and when the truck takes a turn, we go flying. Uncle Jules warns us a couple of times to keep it down. But we're having so much fun it is hard to keep from laughing out loud.

After what seems an eternity we arrive at our destination in Knokke. Uncle Jules opens the door, "Out you come kids," he says with a cheerful voice. He is usually pretty miserable. I wonder why he is so happy all of a sudden. It takes us a while to get used to the sunlight. The house he rented is a large two story house with white bricks. It is only steps away from the white sandy beach. We can see the sea and hear the sound of the surf pounding against the breakwater. We quickly take all the stuff out of the truck and drag it into the house, suitcases, linens, sheets and pillow cases. Now that everything is in the house we all want to go to the beach right away.

Uncle says" Hold on to your horses. Let's go and eat first. I'm kind of hungry and I am sure that you kids could eat a little something too. Am I right?"

"Yea, let's go and eat first." When we walk along the boardwalk we see many restaurants. Uncle picks the one that he likes best. He orders for us all. "Bifsteck and patates frites for everyone," he orders. That's fine with me I love steak and fries. After lunch we rush home, put on our bathing suits and we go to the beach. Folding chairs are set up, but the children have to sit on the sand on big towels. We run into the sea and run right back out. Even though the sun is warm, the water is very cold. We sit around for a while and then we decide we will build a sand castle. Maurice starts by digging a big moat around the castle. This way the water fills the moat without touching the castle. Then we all start piling the sand in the middle. We make a big pile of sand. And that's the way our castle stays. One big pile of sand surrounded by water. Eventually the water creeps into the castle and starts to wash it away. The sun is going down. It's beautiful to see. The sun is like a giant red ball and it looks like it's going to fall into the sea. We go home to eat. I am very hot and dizzy. Aunt Ninon says that we all got sun burned. My skin hurts so much that I can't sleep. Juliana and I are crying because of the pain. Aunt is cooling us down by putting wet towels on our bodies. It cools us down but makes us shiver because now we are cold. We don't sleep most of the night. Near morning we get some relief and we fall asleep, just as it is time to get up. Uncle Jules decides he has to go back to Berchem, because he has to work and he leaves us in Knokke. We have the best time we've ever had, swimming, walking along the beach, searching for seashells. It does not take long to fill a big bag full of shells and we take them back with us. After a few days, something starts to smell in the house and Aunt Ninon says that it is because some of the seashells still have animals inside of them and so she throws them all out. After that, it does not smell anymore. She says, "Don't bring anymore shells home with you." Pretty well every day we eat our meals in restaurants. I eat langoustes for the first time and mussels and patates frites. I have never tasted anything so good. We are not allowed to drink anything with the food because Aunt Ninon says that patates frites and water doesn't mix. I am thirsty, so I sneak some water and luckily, I don't get sick that night.

Aunt Ninon gets sick; we have to take her to the hospital. She is in tremendous pain and she is crying. I guess she must have had some water with her patates frites. Uncle comes back from Berchem and says that she has acute appendicitis and peritonitis. This is when the appendicitis bursts, he explains. The doctors have to operate right away. We all wait in the hospital. After waiting forever, the doctor comes out of the operating room and says that Auntie is fine. She was very lucky. If we had brought her in a moment later she would have died. She has to stay in the hospital for a whole week. We go and visit her every day. She explains how they shove gauze into the opening and how they have to clean out the infection from the peritonitis. Listening to her tell it, gives me a sick feeling in my tummy. At the end of a week we are allowed to take her home. She still has to rest. Uncle stays with her while we kids go to the beach. Raymond, as always, is left in charge of the rest of us kids. He likes to boss us around.

We get some bicycles one day and we ride them up and down the boardwalk all afternoon. Mine is a three-wheeler. We race back and forth but I never win Raymond and Maurice are always faster than I am. I love the sound of the sea at night. I lie in my bed and through the open window. I hear sound of the waves. It is so relaxing it puts me to sleep. This is the best time I've ever had. It's over too soon. One day uncle comes back with the truck. We load everything back into it and we go back to Berchem. We are all really sad and nobody wants to play on the way home. "This has been the best vacation we've ever had." Says Raymond. We all nod.

CHAPTER 26

Uncle Jules is in the fruit business. He sells fruit to fruit stores. He always brings home lots of fruit for us to eat. One day though he tells Aunt Ninon that he has decided to get out of the fruit business and start a flower business selling to flower stores with his partner, Max Bouwman. They buy a Borgward diesel truck and every Tuesday and Thursday, they leave very early in the morning to buy flowers at the auction in Aalsmeer, Holland. During summer vacation he lets me come along. We sit down in the seats in front of the huge auction clock and he tells me to push the button at the back of the chair in front of us. Someone is always ahead of me. Uncle Jules laughs. So the next time the clock starts up I push the button right away as soon as it starts. There is a big commotion from all the people that are sitting there and Uncle says with a red face, "Sorry the kid pushed the button by mistake." Everybody is laughing now, but not me.

"You wanted me to push the button." "shhhhs, be quiet, you'll get us in trouble and then they'll want me to take the load of flowers you bought at the price you bid, which is much too high. You wouldn't that, would you?" I don't care. I am angry now, because everybody is laughing at me and I don't like people laughing at me, especially after I did what he had asked me to do. I can't stay angry for long. It is all so new and exciting, so I enjoy the rest of the day. When the auction is over around noon time all the flowers that Uncle Jules bought are put on big carts and the carts are rolled to an area where they are put in big boxes and then all the boxes are loaded in our truck.

It's long drive home from Aalsmeer to Berchem. We have to cross the border and I get nervous. Uncle Jules always tells me that he is smuggling butter and meat and that I should keep quiet and not say anything about that to the inspector. If he does not want me to say anything why does he tell me that he is smuggling? He should not say anything to me. "Smuggling is bad." I tell him. I'm afraid we'll get put into jail if they find out. He laughs and says it's OK everybody does it. This is the only part of the trip I don't like and I'm always relieved when we have crossed the border.

Once home the flowers are made ready for the trip to Uncle Jules' customers the following morning. We get up very early, around 4am, and start out to be at his first customer by 7am. I am still sleepy and I fall asleep in the truck. He wakes me and tells me that I snore. We arrive at Henrioul's in Hasselt right at seven. I help unload some of the flowers and then we have a steaming cup of coffee with the most delicious homemade bread that Mrs. Henrioul just baked. Laden with butter and homemade jam it tastes better than cake. And so it goes for the whole day from one customer to the next. Everywhere we go the people want us to eat and drink something. At lunchtime, we stop at Madame Bell in Verviers. She has a flower store and her husband runs the Café out of the same place. Outside the café there is a plaque that announces "POMPES FUNEBRES" I don't know what it means, exactly, but I think it has something to do with funerals. Bell's is right across the street from a large cemetery. People come into the café after they come from the cemetery and start to drink and enjoy themselves. I find it very strange. They just came from the cemetery because somebody died. They should be crying, not laughing. Mr. and Mrs. Bell are very nice. She is plump and he is skinny. Mr. Bell has a deep voice and he likes to laugh. His laugh is very loud and deep. They have a son and a daughter. Jean the son helps in the store but his sister Nadine is too young to work. Mrs. Bell gives uncle Jules and me a café filtre. The coffee is very strong, but I like it. We eat the thick slices of bread covered with a thick layer of butter and Gouda cheese that aunt Ninon made for us. It's delicious.

At the end of the day, if there are any unsold flowers, Uncle Jules goes to the flower people at the market and sells all he has left at a very special price. He calls that "los maken" (get rid of). He is happiest when the truck is completely empty and so am I. I am pretty tired by now and I want to go home. It's a long drive. It's been a good day. Uncle has a thick wad of money and he is satisfied

"Jackie we've done well today" he says. "I will give you twenty francs because you were such a big help."

"Thank you uncle," I feel very pleased with myself. He does not speak much to me. I feel special, when he says nice things and does not yell at me.

One day he has a big fight with his partner Max Bouwman and from that moment on they no longer are partners.

Aunt Ninon and uncle Jules insist that I call them Mom and Dad. It is difficult for me. I ask them why my name is Veffer and their name is Nebig.

"If you want me to call you Mom and Dad then I should have the same last name as you have," I say. They say that it is not possible because they are not allowed to adopt me. I don't understand it. How can I call them Mom and Dad if my name is different from theirs? Uncle Jules says that he will get me a golden ring for my seventh birthday and the initials on it will say JN for Jackie Nebig. Excited, because I will finally have the Nebig name I wait for my birthday t come. My seventh birthday falls on October 12. Today is that day. Nobody remembers my special day. I don't say anything to anyone. I am terribly sad and disappointed though. On October 26 Aunt Ninon says,"I think it's your birthday today. Happy birthday Jackie." Although my birthday was a few weeks ago, I say nothing and I am happy that they remember. I wait for my golden ring from uncle Jules. He says that he forgot to get the ring for me but he will get it in the next few days. How can he forget a promise? A promise is a promise. Days turn into weeks and weeks turn into months. I never do get the ring. I learn a hard lesson that people don't keep their promises, and they always forget my birthday. One year later on October 12, on my eighth birthday, I expectantly await congratulations from everyone, but like the previous two years, my birthday is forgotten again. I ask myself, "why is only my birthday forgotten year after year?" They don't forget Juliana's or Raymond's birthdays. The answer I arrive at is that no one cares about me and that is why no one remembers. Months after my birthday and after many promises about the ring, my uncle comes home one day and says "Happy birthday, we got a present for you." I open the ring box to look at the ring inside and the letters that are inscribed on it, I look for the long sought after letters "JN". Cleverly disguised but noticeable only to my discerning eye I see the letters JV. Disappointed, I point this out to uncle Jules.

"No it says JN, Look you can see the J and intertwined is the letter N," he insists. As much as I want to believe him, I can only see JV. This affirms my greatest fear that after all I am not a member of this family. Feeling great guilt about being here, I realize, sadly, that I do not belong here; unfortunately I have nowhere else to go. I try to make the best of it by being as unobtrusive as possible. I love to read. So I read the few books that I have over and over. Speaking is not my strong suit because I don't really want to be noticed. I become an expert at not being seen. I can be in a room full of people and nobody will notice me. It is as if I can make myself invisible. I practice doing that.

CHAPTER 27

One of my very favorite things to do is to go to Antwerp with Uncle. We do many fun things. First, we go grocery shopping at GEBA's, a beautifully appointed store in the Pelikaan Straat. We buy fruit, vegetables, butter and cheese and sometimes ginger in a sweet syrupy juice. I love that. The store also has eau de Cologne, 4711. It smells wonderful. We get some of that too. He gets us lots of candy for treats later on, Rademaker hopjes, Cote D'Or bitter chocolate, zoute drop, griotjes and rock candy. These are all my favourites. I can't wait to eat some of each. After the shopping we go to the barbershop. He gets a shave and a haircut. He tells me I need a haircut also. Uncle wants my hair cut short and I like it long. I don't complain though, because he gets angry very quickly. I am scared of his anger. Once we have had our haircuts we go to a café, Piet Hobeyn, in the Aneeskens straat, off the Keyserlei. Uncle says that Piet Hobeyn is a boxer and that he had won the championship of Europe. I am impressed, though I don't know really why, but if Uncle thinks it is worthwhile for me to know this, it must be really important. I get a Coca Cola to drink and Uncle Jules has a borreltje of Ouwe Klaare. He plays Klabbejas with his friends. He always wins. The loser has to give the winner a box of Godiva chocolates. I like Godiva chocolates. When we're finished we drive home in Uncle's new 1947 Oldsmobile Rocket 88. It is black and has lots of shiny chrome. The car rides so smooth that you hardly know the car is moving. I can stretch out completely on the back seat and go to sleep. Most of the time I like to sit up front next to uncle and watch the traffic. I really like being in the car and I don't want the trip to end.

Sometimes Aunt Ninon goes shopping in Antwerp with us to buy clothes and shoes. Uncle Jules does not like it so we usually go alone with Auntie. Maurice, Raymond Juliana and I are walking hand in hand along the Keyserlei. Someone takes our picture and gives us a card. We pick the picture up on our way back from the store and we give the man some money. When we go to the shoe store, every one of the children gets a new pair.

Auntie asks me," Jackie do your shoes fit you. Do you have room to wiggle your toes?"

"Yes Auntie. Thank you for getting me new shoes." After a while my feet hurt in my new shoes. I dare not complain even though my toes hurt a lot. So I walk around like that until I can get a new pair some many months later.

We walk to the l'Innovation Department store. Auntie gets us new shirts, pants, socks and underwear. Across from the l'Innovation Department Store is a coffee store called Van Ryckstaal and Auntie always gets her coffee there. She buys a blend, Santos and Bourbon, coffee beans. The store smells of coffee and thee and chocolates. For lunch, we go to Rolmops in the Station Straat and we each have Filet Americain Preparé on a crusty roll. It is so good. Sometimes she takes us to the Zoo right next to The Central Station. The highlight in the zoo I find are the monkeys. They are so funny they make me laugh. The gorilla gets mad and takes some of his poop and hurls it at me. Luckily there is a glass between the gorilla and me. The poop makes a loud noise against the glass and scares the living daylights out of me.

When uncle Jules sees how much money she spent he starts to yell"; Ik kom er niet met stelen aan." I don't really know what that means but I gather that he is not pleased that Auntie spent so much on us. I feel guilty.

CHAPTER 28

Today I walk around the house, listless.

Auntie asks," What is the matter with you?"

"Oh, nothing; I just feel weird in my head". She calls the doctor and after he examines me, he confirms that there is definitely something wrong with me. I have scarlet fever and he says it is very contagious and I have to stay in a room all by myself, away from the rest of the family, for six weeks. The windows have to stay closed and I cannot be exposed to drafts. I cannot eat anything that has salt in it. I must stay in bed all that time. So Auntie puts me in one of the large rooms upstairs, all by myself, I am not allowed to wash.

"When you have to go to the bathroom you must do on the potty I will leave in your bedroom. OK. It's very important that you don't leave your room. You don't want to infect everyone in the house with your scarlet fever, do you?"

"Of course not Auntie," horrified at the thought of all of us having to stay in the same room for the next six weeks if I infect everybody. She says that she will check on several times a day. It is boring all day by myself with nothing to do. Auntie comes and visits in the morning when she brings a tray with my breakfast and then once again for lunch and supper. Before she enters my room, she puts on a white lab coat. It makes her look like a doctor. She comes, takes the potty away a few times a day, and replaces it with a clean one. The food tastes awful without salt. She gives me this green soup and she says it is parsley soup. "You'll like it" she says. I hate it. It has no taste.

One day auntie says,"You can get up for a little while, stand by the window, and wave at Juliana and Maurice." They are waving up at me from outside on the street. The sun is shining. I can feel the warmth of the sun through the glass. How I wish I could play with them.

"Soon enough you'll be all better and then you can go outside again," she assures me.

"Can you bring me my books to read? She brings me several books. Pretty soon I lose myself in the wonderful world of Pietje Bell. The day finally arrives when I am no longer sick and the first thing Auntie does is to give me a warm bath. I guess all those weeks without washing did not improve my smell much. When I leave the room, I have to leave everything that I wore inside the room and put new clean clothes on, outside of the room. Eating regular food again has never tasted better. A company comes to disinfect the room and they seal the door all around with tape.

"Leave it like that for a week," they say. "After that you can unseal the room" The disinfectant smells terrible and makes me want to vomit. The doctor says that I am OK.

"One of the after effects of scarlet fever is that you can go deaf or loose some of your eyesight," he says. Sure enough after a while, I can't see the blackboard in class. I squint and through the slits in my eyes I manage to see what is written on the board. I have to start wearing glasses to improve my eyesight.

Aunt Ninon loves fresh air. While we are asleep, she always opens the windows wide, even in the middle of winter. The bedrooms are not heated and in the morning when we get up the floors are stone cold. So we get our clothes on as quickly as we can and we flee the room to the kitchen where it's warm. By now auntie has lit the stove and the coffee is brewing. The kitchen is the one place where the entire family gathers, in the winter. It is warm and cozy and Aunt Ninon tells stories about her time in prison in Breendonk. Uncle Jules never talks about his time in prison. When Auntie starts to tell her stories he prefers not to listen and walks away to the front room. She tells us, in a proud voice, that Juliana was born while she was in prison on July 27, 1942. Why should that make her proud?

She tells Maurice and me that we have to go for a walk every day. "The fresh air will do you good." She yells after us when we're outside. Maurice has trouble with breathing because of his asthma and I have weak lungs. We have our favourite walk, Maurice and I. We imagine that we are on an adventure and we conquer this great land, somewhere far away. The people await our coming to make them free and when we finally arrive there is a great rejoicing. People cheer and music plays and we ride in a parade, waving benevolently to everyone along the way. That is when we get to the second park on our walk. In the first park we passed we had to slay dragons and overcome the poisoned air that makes it hard to breath. Maurice always leads the charge on his big white horse and I am happy to follow, after all it is his wonderful story that we are living. It's getting late and we have to get back in time for supper. Auntie gets very mad if we arrive home late. We get back just before dark and Maurice and I are flushed with excitement for once again we saved the world from tyranny. I love Maurice, he always looks after me, because that's what he promised to Mommy and Daddy, and we have the greatest adventures together. So long as I'm with him nothing bad can happen to me. Mommy and Daddy will come to get us. They are probably looking for us right now. I know it. Even though Aunt and Uncle are saying that they will not be back because they died in a concentration camp, I feel that they are rich and living somewhere in America. They will find us.

CHAPTER 29

It is 1948. I read my New Years message to Mom and Dad and this year I promised that I will be extra nice to them. I have finally gotten used to calling Aunt Ninon and Uncle Jules, Mom and Dad. They really seem to like that and I don't mind anymore, so long as they are nice to me. I feel safe and comfortable with them. I think they must love me by now. I have to make them feel like I love them too. I do well in school I am always obedient, I clean my room and I hardly ever get into trouble. That seems to please them immensely. They always hold me up as an example in front of Maurice. "Why can't you be like your brother, Jackie, he is so smart? I hate it when they do that. Maurice is smart; they just don't give him a chance. No matter what he does to please them; they are always cross with him. I am sad when they do that. Can't they see that he is also a good boy like me?

***

There is trouble in Germany again. Like the whole of Germany, Berlin is divided into four occupied zones, under the jurisdiction of the Allied Control Council, France, Great Britain, the United Sates and the Soviet Union. Berlin is within Soviet-occupied East Germany. France Great Britain and The United States decide to unite their occupied zones by creating a single new Deutsche Mark in West Germany as well as in West Berlin. Stalin sees this as a threat to the East German economy and in June 1948 the Soviet forces begin a blockade of all rail, road, and water traffic through East Germany to West Berlin, thereby trying to push the western powers out of the city of Berlin. The United States and Great Britain react by sending food and other vital supplies into the city by air. Tensions build up as extra troops are sent into the occupied zones. The Soviets finally end the blockade after the West sets up an embargo on exports from East Germany.

***

No matter how careful I am I break my glasses at least once a month. I am scared to go home to face Mom and Dad, because they will yell at me. When I get home they don't notice that I am not wearing my glasses and I start to relax. The next day Mom asks me "Why are you not wearing you glasses?" I tell her I broke them. She is not even a little bit mad at me. This confuses me. It's not like her not to get upset. Usually she yells her head off. She laughs and says,"Boys will be boys." She tells me to go around the corner on the Diksmuide Laan to get a new pair. Relieved, I take the money she hands me and run over to the Optician and wait while he fixes me a new pair exactly the same as the old pair.

I am reading a new book I got from St. Nicholas called "The Scheepsjongens van Bontekoe" by Johan Fabricius. The book is very thick and as I start reading my vivid imagination transports me to the ship of Captain Willem Ysbrantsz Bontekoe. What wonderful adventures I have on one of the ships of the "Verenigde Oostindische Compagnie". The ship is on its way to West India via the Cape of Good Hope. Johan Fabricius speaks to the heart of every boy"The life of a man, my boys, never passes without storms. The further you want to sail the more difficult and dangerous the trip." Though I am but a boy I've traveled long and far and it's been difficult and dangerous and stormy. Today I feel like a man.

Kindervreugd arranges for the kids in our school to attend live theater productions. The live performances are both glorious and uplifting and. We are invited to attend to the theater about once every month. Sometimes they have musical concerts. A symphony orchestra will play perform music by Mozart or Schubert or Peter and the Wolf by Prokokief. We also have the opportunity to experience ballet performances, not really my favourite.

Mom says,"In order to have a well rounded education; you must be exposed to all forms of artistic expression. Next we will take you to see a Puccini opera." Oh boy, I can't wait.

***

Ever since the end of the war Belgium has experienced a political crisis over the way King Leopold III, Belgium's king, conducted himself and the affairs of the country during the war. We learn about current events in school and the teacher goes to great length to explain the fine details about the current King, Leopold III. People are holding protest marches and there is a general sense of unease over his continued reign. Some accuse him of collaborating with the Germans. Since his ancestry is from Germany it is a plausible story. In 1936, King Leopold announces a fundamental change in foreign policy; Belgium abandons its military alliance with France in favour of a return to neutrality. Belgium has always been considered a buffer state wedged between the two antagonists, Germany and France. The cancellation of the alliance is viewed as a concession to the Germans to help them facilitate access to France. In May 1940, Germany, which in 1937 had guaranteed Belgian neutrality, invaded Belgium and Holland. Leopold leads the Belgian army in a weak resistance to the Germans. After the defense becomes hopeless, Leopold, over the opposition of his cabinet, surrenders unconditionally, thus provoking accusations of treason. The German authorities hold him as a prisoner of war at his castle at Laken. Leopold, to his credit, does not want to exercise an active rule under German scrutiny. After his first wife, Astrid, was killed in an automobile accident, while Leopold was at the wheel, he marries a commoner, whom he later made the princess of Réthy. Princess Astrid was well loved by the Belgian people and they always blamed Leopold for her death. Leopold was removed to Germany in 1944, and subsequently freed by Allied troops in 1945. His return to Belgium was a burning political issue. The Liberal and leftist parties accuse him of cooperating with Nazi Germany and of fascist sympathies. His support comes mainly from the Catholic Conservatives. In 1945, Leopold is barred from returning without the permission of the parliament. He spends his exile mostly in Switzerland while his brother, Prince Charles, acts as regent. A referendum is held in 1950 favouring the king's return by a slight majority. However, Leopold's arrival in Belgium is followed by such unrest that he transfers the royal powers to his eldest son, Baudouin, In July 1951, Leopold formally abdicates.

***

CHAPTER 30

Mom calls me. She is in bed and she has a fever. I am the only one home. She wants a glass of water and a cool, damp cloth to put on her head. I run to get her the things she requested. She looks very pale. I put the cloth on her head and I put the glass to her mouth. She tries to drink but she is too weak to swallow. I wish someone would come home now. They'd know what to do. I don't know. I am only ten years old. Raymond, Maurice and Juliana arrive home; they've been grocery shopping for tonight's meal. Normally I would have gone with them but not today because I am reading the best part of my book. The part where Captain Bontekoe's ship blows up by accident. I quickly tell Raymond that Mom is sick and in bed. He does not know what to do either. Then Maurice has the bright idea to call Doctor Doge. Raymond dials the number and talks to the doctor's wife and she takes down the information. "The doctor will come out later tonight," she says. Dad is not home; he usually does not get home until 8:00pm. We don't know his whereabouts or how to get a hold of him. Maria, the woman that comes and cleans the house, has already gone home for the day. So we sit and we wait for Doctor Doge to arrive. I feel a little easier now since everyone else shares the worry of taking care of Mom.

At about seven the doorbell rings and it is the doctor. He'll know what to do. We all go into Mom's room.

"All of you, out, I have to examine your mother and I can't do that with all of you standing around here." After what seems an eternity he comes out and he has a concerned look on his face. "Where is your father?" he asks.

"He is on the road visiting his customers. He'll probably be home by eight tonight," says Raymond. Doctor Doge gives Raymond his card and says "Have your father give me a phone call as soon as he gets home. Good night" and by this he leaves. We all pile back in Mom's room. She is lying in bed. She does not look well, very pale and she is too weak to say anything. No one utters a word for fear of disturbing her. We stand around until Dad arrives home. We're all talking at the same time "Mom is sick the doctor wants you to call him right away.

" Hold it, one at the time I can't hear a thing you kids are saying." So Raymond is the spokesman, since he is the oldest, and explains the situation. Dad runs into the bedroom to survey the situation with his own eyes. He phones the doctor and he tells him that Mom probably has TB. She has to go to the hospital for a chest X-ray in the morning. The doctor already made the appointment. The test comes back positive. She has TB. The very first effective treatment for Tuberculosis is provided by health resorts called sanitariums, so Dad makes arrangements to take her to a Sanitarium in Davos, Switzerland. Patients at a sanitarium are given bed rest, fresh air and mild exercise. People can live a long life even with the bacteria, and who knows; in the future medicine may find a cure for the dreaded disease. In the meantime Maria, the woman that cleans the house, is left in charge. We all like Maria; she does not have a husband so she stays over at our house at night and takes care of our needs in the morning, preparing breakfast, lunches and supper. She cleans the house when she feels like it. It isn't as if someone is supervising her. She loves to eat sandwiches with butter and lots of salt.

"That's not good for you Maria," says Raymond.

"Mind your own business young man" is her reply as she continues to munch on her salty treat.

Doctor Doge comes one day and says that we all have to have a TB skin test done to see if we react positive or negative to the Tuberculosis bacteria. The next day we all go to the doctor's office and each of us gets three scratches on our arms and Doc puts some stuff on each scratch. The following day my arm is really swollen and red and I feel horribly sick.

"Maria I want to stay in bed. I am way to sick to get up," I say in a feeble voice.

"No Jackie you got to get up, you'll feel better when you walk around," and with this Maria pulls off the covers and makes me get out of bed.

The other children, Juliana, Maurice and Raymond are fine. Maria commands in a strident voice,"Lets all go to the beach for the day." I want to kill her because her voice gives me an instant piercing headache. I don't want to go. She takes me anyway. I am so bloody sick all day that I can't do anything. I have never felt so bad in all my life. When we get home, I am so relieved because now I can go to bed.

For the next few days, I can barely muster the strength to go to the bathroom, let alone go to school. After the third day, I start to feel better. By the end of the week, I am OK again. The doctor tells dad that the TB Bacillus, he calls it the Koch Bacillus, is dormant in my body and that I should be fine. In the meantime, the doctor says that dad should find a place somewhere in the country, where the air and the climate is better for Mom away from the big city. So dad starts to look for a house in Kapellenbos, outside of Antwerp. He finds a beautiful villa and he buys it. He visits Mom on a regular basis. Apparently she is staying in a pretty fancy sanatorium. There are famous people there from all over the world. There is an American movie actor and the prime minister of Siam, says dad. Mom is doing well. It's been six months. She is now ready to come home. We're all pretty excited. We are moving into our new house in the country and Mom is coming home.

CHAPTER 31

At school I have to tell Freddie that we are leaving to go to another town and another school. "Goodbye Freddie, I'll never forget you. You'll come and visit me and I'll visit you regularly. OK." I'm so sad I feel like crying. We swear to each other that we will stay in touch. It is hard to say goodbye. I will miss this school. I have grown to like it and my teachers. The day arrives when we have to move from Berchem to Kapellenbos. A big truck arrives one morning and all the furniture is loaded. Dad has another new car. He just took delivery of a 1950 Oldsmobile 88 Hydramatic. Dad is the only one that has seen the house. We have not seen it yet. It's a long drive. The drive takes us along tree lined roads and green pastures. It sure is pretty. I've not been in the country before; we have always lived in a big city.

When we arrive at the new house, it is much bigger than I imagined. It is a large three-story house, completely whitewashed and it has a red tiled roof. It even has a name "Villa Den Linden." The yard is immense with a very large front gate. We can also get to the house through the back lane. That is where the garage is located. Entering the house at the rear entrance reveals a big laundry room and a washroom. From there we enter into a huge kitchen. When we open the door on the right, we enter into a large formal dining room. A huge crystal chandelier hangs from the ceiling. The floors are made of beautiful dark stained parquet. The dinning room is adjoined by the large living room that has a huge fireplace. The ceilings are composed of gleaming, large wooden beams that stretch the entire length of the rooms. On the second floor, there are four bedrooms and a large bathroom and on the third floor, there are two more bedrooms. I never imagined that our new house would be so large.

The following day Dad takes us to our new school to be registered. All of us kids will be attending the same school. It goes from Grade 1 to Grade 12. I will enter grade 5. Maurice and Raymond will enter grade 8 and Juliana will be in Grade 3. The school is named the "Athenaeum of Kapellen." The complex of school buildings was at one time the large estate of a very wealthy family in Kapellen. The grounds where the children go for recess were once the gardens of the estate. It contains exquisite flowers and rhododendrons and acacia trees. The children are not allowed to touch the flowers or harm the bushes. We are told that they are there to make the school more beautiful. I can't wait to start school.

Mom arrives home today from Switzerland. We all are told that we have to be on our best behaviour and take care of Mom's every need. Dad went by plane to Switzerland to get her. They travel back together on the plane. Mom looks good after being away for more than six months. She put on some weight and her cheeks are rosy. She wears glasses now. I never noticed her glasses before. They must be new. She quit smoking and she says," Now it is dad's turn to stop." They both smoked "ARO Jaune". Stinky cigarettes that make the air smoky and make me cough even though I don't smoke them. Dad gets mad. He says, "I don't want to stop, I enjoy smoking, and it relieves my tension." I want to do things for Mom, but I don't know what to do or where to start so I just stand around and wait for her to ask me to do something. She stays in bed most of the day. Doctor's orders. We have a new woman that comes and cleans the house every day and cooks for us. Her name is Louise. She is married. Her husband is Gus and he is a bicycle road racer. That's his job. He is not very good at it, so on the side he is also a barber. He trains every day on a standing bike. He says to me "Here you try it" I try it for the first time and I fall off the bike. The second time I manage to stay on. The seat's too high so I can't sit on the seat. I have to stand on the pedals and ride that way. It's not easy and not very comfortable.

Gus says, "We should do some road racing"

"That would be nice but I don't have a bike."

"Maybe your Dad will get you one for your birthday."

Gus has very interesting stories about different road races he's been in. I love listening to him. He gets me interested in the "Tour de France" the longest bicycle road race in the world. Every day we listen together to the races and the results. He wants the Belgian Rick van Steenbergen to win, but deep in my heart I want Italy's Fausto Coppi to win. I imagine myself being in the races and racing against Gino Bartali, Stan Ockers, Louison Bobet, Fausto Coppi and Rick van Steenbergen.

Dad, surprises me one day, when he announces that he is taking me to see the soccer game between Holland and Belgium. The competition between these two teams has always been fierce, not a quarter is given on either side and that's the way the fans love it. There is no love lost between the Belgians and the Dutch. The Dutch call the Belgians "Patates frites vreeters" (French Fries eaters) and the Belgians call the Dutch, "Kaaskoppen" (Cheese heads). Both sides perceive these labels as great insults, even though they sound quite innocuous enough. But it's in the way that these insulting names are delivered, therein lays the great insult. The Dutch staunchly support their men in orange and the Belgians just as fiercely support their team. It makes for a hard fought and exciting rivalry between the two teams. As a Dutch person living in Belgium I don't know which side to root for. I have mixed emotions about it. In the end I favour Holland as my team. We get to Antwerp and find our seats. This is the first International game I have ever attended and I feel pretty special. I recognize the names of many of the Belgian players, Jeff Mermans from Anderlecht, Rick Coppens from Beerschot, Jim Vanderven from Berchem, and so on. Anderlecht is currently the best soccer team in Belgium. It has won the championship in its division for the last three years in a row. The only players I know on the Dutch team are Abe Lenstra, Piet Kraak and Faas Wilkes. I immerse myself in the game. The Dutch are famous for their singing of "Oranje Boven" (Orange is tops). The noise in the Stadium is deafening and to my chagrin the Belgians win the game 2-0. Dad is happy because he roots for the Belgian side. Nevertheless I have to admit that I really enjoyed the game and I look forward to see another one in the next few months. The next one will be played at Feyenoord stadium in Rotterdam. Dad promises he will take me.

Juliana has a friend down the street, his name is Eddie. Sometimes I go and play with Eddie and Juliana. One day we decide to play doctor and we all get undressed and we start examining each other. Eddie tells his mother and she comes over to our house and screams at Mom and Dad at the top of her voice for a while. Then she takes off in a huff.

"We're in trouble now" I say to Juliana. Mom and Dad just stand there and laugh till the tears are running down their cheeks. We don't understand what's going on. All they say is, "You better don't go over to Eddie's anymore." I'll never understand grownups. When I think they should not be mad, they get mad. And at times like these when I think we're in deep trouble they just laugh.

Dad got me an exciting new book "Om het bruine Monster" It is a soccer book written by Pieter Nierop about two young boys, Roel Boontje Bontebal and Bul Barendse, that organize a soccer team in their native Polderdam in Holland. The two actually make it to the Dutch National team and go on to beat an Italian team. It is so exciting to read and I imagine myself at all the games. I want to join a soccer team and tell Mom.

She does not like it and she tells me,"remember you have weak lungs, you had Pleurisy and Pneumonia and you also have the TB bacteria in you, so I don't think you should play organized soccer."

"I'll be careful Mom, please let me play," I cry. She relents

"OK, but be careful and when you get tired make sure you tell coach to take you off."

"Yes mom, thanks mom". And off I go to the clubhouse where Heidebos, the local soccer team plays and I sign up. They give me a jersey, shorts and socks. The coach tells me to come back to practice the following week Tuesday with my own shin pads and soccer boots.

"And get the authorization form signed." He yells after me as I depart. I tell Dad, because I know he likes soccer and does not mind it if I play. He signs the required form and he takes me to the store and gets the shin pads and the best boots.

"If you're going to play soccer, you might as well play the best you can, so you need the best equipment." He tells me knowingly.

"Dad, come and watch me practice,"

"If I can I will," he promises. He never makes it to any of my games or practices. I turn out to be one of the better players on the team and I score many goals. It really does not matter because nobody ever comes to watch me play and I can't share my triumph with anyone.

Coach calls me in one day after a game and says that he wants to use me on his traveling team. I am elated, that's quite a distinction. Not too many kids get promoted to the traveling team.

Coach says, " Ask your parents if it's OK and bring me back the form, signed by your father or mother." I can't wait to get home and tell Mom and Dad the good news. Dad is not home yet so I tell mom.

Her answer is unequivocal,"Definitely not, you cannot play on the traveling team, it will tire you out too much and it's not good for your weak lungs. I forbid you to play anymore soccer"

"All right I'll continue in the house league."

"No I don't want you to play soccer anymore.

I am utterly devastated. How can she do this? Does she not know that soccer is most important in my life? I speak with Dad when he comes home and he says that he thinks I could continue to play soccer but that I have to convince Mom.

"I'll put in a good word, don't worry," he promises. In the meantime, I have to give coach the news that I can no longer play soccer.

"Do you want me to come and talk to your mother?" "

"No, that will make matters worse" I reply. "I'll have to convince her by myself." I am not good at pleading my own case, and in the end I lose out. I've become used to losing so I don't get that upset over it anymore. Sometimes I think, though, it's not fair. Why do all good things that happen have to end? I had my own

Mommy and Daddy. I had them and then they left, never to return. Maurice he comes and goes. He is with me for a while and then he leaves for a long time. Then there is Earl my Canadian soldier friend he went back to his country. My aunt Saar and Uncle Jonas and their kids. I liked it a lot with them. Uncle Levie, Auntie Roo and their son Loukie, Judith and Jopie Dinsdag, Aunt Dora and Uncle Kees, Aunt Miep and Uncle Louis, Aunt Bora and Uncle Harry, Marain and Parain. I was with all of them for a while, but nobody seemed to like me enough to keep me with them. Now with Aunt Ninon and Uncle Jules they'll probably want to get rid of me eventually. I've learned never to get too attached to people. People come and go.

We go for long walks in the woods. Where we live, forests, mostly pine trees, tall acacias, chestnut trees and lots of rhododendrons, surround us. Dad bought us a dog, a German Sheppard named Duke. I have to walk him every day on the leach. When he gets off the leach, he takes off and won't return till hours later. Dad beats to make him listen but nothing seems to help. He is a runner. I don't like taking Duke for walks because he pulls so hard I can barely contain him. I kick him in the butt to get his attention. He carries right on pulling. We took him to obedience school. The teacher told us our dog was too stupid to learn anything. Duke was not with us for long. He was sick, he had cancer of the testicles and he had to be put down. We loved our stupid dog, Duke. Now I walk by myself, usually with Juliana in tow. She insists on tagging along. I toss pebbles along the way, trying to hit the trees. One pebble gets away from me and hits her in the head. She wails so loud I get scared. I look at her head; I can't see anything, no blood or cuts. She promises that she won't tell Mom about the accident. We pick Chanterelles mushrooms. They are yellow and they are flat on top, the edges are uneven. They have a pleasant smell. Chanterelles are only found in the wild. Efforts to cultivate Chanterelles have never proven successful. Tough mild, Chanterelles have a slight spicy edge which is characteristic of things that grow on their own in the forest, something that comes from competing in a natural environment I guess. At home, Mom fries them in butter with salt and pepper they are delicious on a slice of bread. Then Juliana tells Mom that I hit her in the head with a rock, on purpose, no less. If stares could kill, she would be dead for sure. After I get yelled at for a half an hour I have to apologize to Juliana. Feeling a sense of betrayal I harbour a vengeful feeling in my heart.

"You wait I'll get even with you" I promise her.

Just as we thought that dad was finished with dogs he brings home another. This time it is a Bouvier puppy. It's so cute. After about six months this dog, fully grown, stands three feet tall. When he puts his paws on my shoulders he is taller than I am. He does not like us kids much. He is forever biting.

"It's all in good fun," Mom says. My arms are black and blue from the bites. She says we need to keep him busy. That means forever walking the beast or playing with him when he is at home. Just so that he won't eat the entire house. Suddenly he bites someone's lip and almost tears it off. That's the end of the Bouvier. After being threatened with a lawsuit, Dad is through with bringing dogs home.

"They're too much trouble" he says.

I have a friend who lives on our street. His name is Erik Elst. He goes to the Athenaeum like most of the other kids. It's the only school in the area. He is in the 7th grade. There aren't any boys my age in the neighbourhood so he and I play together. We play marbles and he beats me most times. I hate to lose and I hate him for winning. Sometimes I get so angry that I start to cry. He thinks it's funny and laughs. Now I hate him even more. Erik's mother is a piano teacher and she taught her son to play. He is great. He plays polonaises by Chopin and Rachmaninof—Piano Concerto No. 2 in C Minor Op. 18 and Listsz' Liebestraum. I can listen to him play for hours. Sometimes he comes over to our house and plays on our piano. At night, when our windows are open and Erik play at his piano, we hear the unmistakable sound of Chopin's "Revolutionaire" waft over the night breezes. It sounds so romantic and Mom loves it. She wants me to start taking piano lessons. So I learn to read music and playing scales, endlessly. Getting sick of playing Czerny's piano exercises, I yearn to play Chopin.

"When do I get to play Chopin and Listsz?"

"Later" Madame Elst promises. She lets me play Beethoven's Fur Elise, Bocherini's Minuet, Schumann's the Happy Farmer and lots of Mozart.

"Chopin and Liszt come much later" she says. When Erik plays Chopin I get shivers up and down my spine. I imagine it is I playing in front of a big audience. Everyone applauds when I finish. I play the Minute Waltz as an encore. It feels wonderful to be adored by your audience. Erik tells me about the piano competition between the Russian Vladimir Ashkenazi and the American Van Cliburn. We both listen to their flawless performances; I suggest that Van Cliburn is the better pianist, however to my surprise Vladimir wins the competition.

Erik is forever experimenting. He has a chemical kit and he decides to manufacture Chlorine. It stinks and it constricts my throat. My fear is that one day he'll blow us both up. Erik's mother has a nickname for him. She calls him Muske. (Little bird). There is an apple orchard next to where he lives has. We sneak into the yard and climb in the trees fill our pockets with apples. We eat as many as we can. They are not ripe yet, they taste awful and I get a stomachache. The next day I'm on the toilet and promise myself I'll never steal those stinky, wormy apples again.

Erik's dad is a wonderful organist. He plays the organ at the big Catholic Church in the village. We're allowed to go along when he practices. The sound reminds me of the time I was in the big Cathedral in Brussels with Marain and Parain. It's amazing how Erik's dad can play the organ as well as he does. He only has three fingers on his right hand. Erik will become a famous Astronomer in Belgium.

CHAPTER 32

They teach Catechism at school. It is not obligatory to take the course, but all the catholic kids take it. Father Paul teaches. It's kind of strange for me to think of a priest as a father. I decide that I want to take Catechism, without telling Mom and Dad that I am doing so. It's interesting to find out the stories from the bible. Father Paul says that we only should read the New Testament, not the Old Testament. Father Paul tells the story of the Good Samaritan. He is a fascinating story teller and everyone is spellbound: "When the Jews of the southern kingdom of Judah returned from their exile in Babylon they looked upon the Samaritans as people who were inferior and had no place in the land of Israel, or any part in God's Kingdom. They didn't let the Samaritans help in re-building the Temple, they didn't associate with Samaritans, and even the word Samaritan was sometimes used as an insult, as those who opposed Jesus Christ blasphemously said to Him: "Are we not right in saying that you are a Samaritan and have a demon?" (John 8:48) "But he, desiring to justify himself, said to Jesus, "And who is my neighbor?" "Jesus replied, "A man was going down from Jerusalem to Jericho, and he fell among robbers, who stripped him and beat him, and departed, leaving him half dead. Now by chance a priest was going down that road; and when he saw him he passed by on the other side. So likewise a Levite, when he came to the place and saw him, passed by on the other side. But a Samaritan, as he journeyed, came to where he was; and when he saw him, he had compassion, and went to him and bound up his wounds, pouring on oil and wine; then he set him on his own beast and brought him to an inn, and took care of him. And the next day he took out two denarii's and gave them to the innkeeper, saying,

'Take care of him; and whatever more you spend, I will repay you when I come back.'" "Which of these three, do you think, proved neighbor to the man who fell among the robbers?" "He said, "The one who showed mercy on him." "And Jesus said to him, "Go and do likewise." (Luke 10:25-37).

The story creates in me a deep emotional impact. How different the attitude of an outcast towards one weak and in need of help as opposed to the disdaining attitude of them that hold the reins of power. There assuredly is a lesson here. At home we don't ever read the bible. Or discuss religion. Father Paul knows that I am Jewish and he is flattered that I take his class. He gives me a small bible as a gift. Reading some of the stories gives me a better understanding of religion. Though the text is largely unintelligible, many of the stories therein are powerful. The stories are probably not meant to be interpreted literally but as examples of how we as human beings should behave towards each other. Father Paul says that we should not get ahead of him and that he will help us interpret the stories as he covers them in class. I decide to read ahead and not wait for him. He won't let us read stories from the Old Testament and I wonder why. I take Catechism for the entire school year. When I get my report card I see that I scored perfect marks in Catechism. I am reluctant to show my report card to Mom and Dad for fear that they will be angry with me for taking a religion class. What is puzzling, when they look over the report they don't comment at all on the mark for religion. I don't say anything about it either. Because I dared rummage in the bin of religious enquiry my interest is forever peaked. I get more than I bargained for, however, as it exposes the malignant underbelly of hatred and derision towards the Jews. The Christian tolerance towards Jews has always been fragile. It resembles contempt, not acceptance. The tolerance stems from the fact that we're kindred People of the Book. I quit the class the following year, not able to cope with the subterfuge, much to the consternation of father Paul.

Mom is forever angry with Maurice. No matter how hard he tries, and God knows he tries hard; he can't seem to do anything right in her eyes. He wants so much to please her. He is forever being punished for one thing or another. She makes fun of him, calls him stupid and makes him feel bad about himself. When the school year ends, Mom tells him he can no longer go to school. Maurice is pretty upset. He wants to continue to get a formal education.

Mom says "If you don't like it here, why don't you write your auntie Saar and Uncle Jonas, they live in Canada now, and see if you can live with them." He sits down and writes them a letter in his best handwriting. We both go into the village to post the letter at the post office. Several weeks go by and one day Maurice receives the long awaited reply to his letter. He opens the letter with great anticipation. Auntie Saar invites him to come and live with them in Canada. He is very happy about the prospect of going to Canada.

"What's going to happen to me, when you're gone?" I ask very worried about the prospect of being on my own without Maurice's support. He does not know how much I need him.

"You'll come and visit me in Canada and one day I'll be back to get you. We'll live in Canada together.

"Promise" I sob with an air of expectant hope in my voice.

"I promise." I think he really means it. I feel somewhat better. It takes him six months to obtain an immigration visa. The day arrives when we have to say goodbye. Dad and I drive Maurice to Antwerp, where the ship is docked, that will take him to Halifax, Canada. We drive in complete silence all the way to Antwerp. Once we get to the docks it's not difficult to find the ship he will sail on. It's an old freighter, rusty in places, and Maurice will be working on the ship for his passage. The trip will last 14 days. I hug him. I don't want him to go.

"Don't cry Jackie, remember what I promised you" Feeling forsaken I let my anguish engulf me. He waves as I watch him go up the gangplank to embark on this strange and wonderful adventure in a far-off country. How I wish I could go with him. He is all of 15 years old.

CHAPTER 33

It never gets really cold in Kapellenbos even in the dead of winter. However, the winter of 1953 is one of the coldest since they started keeping track of these things. The pond across the street has frozen over. The bravest amongst us venture onto the ice, with me watching from a safe distance on shore. Some of the boys jump up and down on the ice in the middle of the pond. The ice holds.

"Come on guys, the ice is OK," yells one of the brave ones. For a while longer we watch cracks develop wondering when one of the boys will finally go through the ice. About a half an hour or so later, the last of us still standing on the side, venture onto the ice surface. It holds. So we all don our ice skates. Mine are borrowed. They are the type you attach to your shoes. They are called Friesche doorlopers (Friesche speed skates). The blades are very long and they are meant to be used in endurance races held on the canals in Holland. I look rather funny with them on. Attempting to play hockey with them is quite a challenge. I've never played before and my skating is not particularly good. After about one hour or so, I get the hang of it. I've got to get a hockey stick though. I find myself a stick in the woods nearby. The stick seems to have enough of a curve on it that makes it useable for a hockey stick. It does not look too bad and it's better than having no stick at all. We don't have a hockey puck so we play with a tennis ball. There are many players so we play ten a side. All are on the ice at the same time. We're having a ball. Shoes are used as hockey nets. It's difficult to score especially since the nets keep getting moved. Once I have a breakaway. I'm all by myself in front of the goalie and I shoot the ball square into the face of the goalie. He falls backwards and the ball trickles in. I'm pretty proud of myself, having scored my first goal. Then my pride turns into concern, I've knocked the goalie unconscious with my shot. Everybody gathers around. The boy soon comes to. We're all relieved. I apologize to the boy. He grins and says,"Boy you've got a wicked shot; maybe I should have stopped it with my hand instead of my face." He's got an angry looking bruise on his forehead, but good- humouredly he insists on playing on. Immediately I take a liking to him. His name is Luc Kiekens and we become the best of friends. From then on, we are inseparable. Luc lives in the villa behind ours in the back lane. He lives there with his father and mother. He's an only child.

Luc comes over one day to meet our family, his parents come with him. They introduce themselves and a friendship evolves. Mom and Dad are invited there for supper. They accept the invitation. While they are there, they also meet the Van Emden's, Maurice and Lucy. The three couples become inseparable friends. Mr. van Emden owns a magazine he publishes called Bolero. It is a "girly" magazine, with lots of pictures of semi-clad girls. He is always the target of the wrath of the Catholic preachers who bemoan the fact that we have a pornographer within our midst that will lead us all to hell and damnation. Every so often people carry placards in front of his house exposing him as a scourge to society. He just thinks it's funny and good for his business. The more they attack him the more people will want to read his magazine, he figures. Mrs. Van Emden, when Mr. van Emden isn't home, makes a fuss over Luc and me. She likes touching us. Usually, when she does her hand lingers a little long over erotic places on our bodies. I don't like to go there when she is alone.

Luc likes to race his bicycle. His has a Peugeot three speed with a racing seat and racing handlebars. It's a sleek streamlined machine. The envy of all the kids in the neighbourhood. In comparison my bike is a nondescript one speed with straight handlebars. I just got it the week before because I was first in my class. I cherish my first bike although I am somewhat envious of Luc's three speed. He imagines he is Stan Ockers, the famous Belgian road racer. He says that I am Rick Van Steenbergen. Luc has a vivid imagination and likes to take charge. He is three years older than I am. So I let him. He always stages the race by announcing in a loud announcer's voice which étape of the Tour de France we are riding in.

"This is the first stage, Paris to Strasbourg" he says, "Stan Ockers is leading the peleton with his team mate Rick Van Steenbergen and both of them escape from the peleton." And with this we both take off standing on our pedals. We ride like this for a few kilometers and then he decides that the end of the race is in sight. We both sprint for the finish line; he is older and stronger and has a better bike so he always beats me in the sprint. Raising both his arms in victory as he crosses the imaginary line he relishes the win. When we don't race our bikes we usually play soccer. We're evenly matched there because I am very good for my age, better than most good. I am glad I can beat him at something. During the long summer vacation, we are together nearly every day. Today we are racing our bikes in Heide. Of course he won again and is enjoying the moment by carrying on talking to the imaginary crowd. I follow him in a rather disconsolate mood and as I try to avoid a pedestrian I hit the curb with my front wheel causing me to flip over my bike. I hit my head on the pavement and my knee hits the edge of the curb. I can feel something crack inside my knee. It's too painful to get up but. I lay there for a while and Luc comes over, looks at me with a concerned look

"Are you all right."

"Of course I am not alright," I scream. "I can't get up. Go get help." A small crowd has now formed around me and everyone is offering their opinions.

"Yep, the knee is definitely broken." Says one. "

"Don't be silly, it's just sprained." Says another "We're definitely going to have to amputate above the knee." Quips a man. Everybody laughs but I am not amused and I glare at the man. "What an idiot. I am in pain and this guy wants to be a comedian at my expense," I think to myself. With Luc's help I manage to get up. My right knee is badly swollen by now and it's turning blue. I hobble on one leg and Luc supports me on the other side. This way we get home. When we reach home after about 30 minutes, Mom has a worried look on her face when she sees the condition of my knee. She immediately phones the doctor. He promises to drop over in about two hours. Mom puts me to bed and gives me something for the pain. She scolds Luc for having caused this accident. Luc goes home feeling guilty. For once I agree with Mom, if he had not raced again then I would not have fallen. I'm glad I can blame him. The doctor comes and says that I have to have complete rest

" We don't want any infection in there." After a week my knee is badly infected. He has to drain the fluid. It's painful and the knee is not healing very well. Luc visits me every day after school. After a month I am still not able to walk. The knee is still blue and it seems to be spreading. The doctor talks quietly to Mom and tells her that unless the swelling goes down and the infection goes away, the knee could become gangrenous. I know what that means, we just learned about gangrene in school. They may have to cut my leg off. I start to cry, I'm really worried now.

The doctor says;"now, now, we won't let that happen. I will prescribe you some penicillin and that will take care of the infection." Sure enough after a week the swelling goes down and the infection is thankfully disappearing. I can now get up and walk around. The pain is almost all gone. Mom says, "Don't hit your knee on anything." I am very careful for the next month. Soon I forget about the mishap. I bang it on several occasions and it does swell up. I am scared to tell mom so I limp around for a month or so and then it's OK again. I breathe a sigh of relief.

Some days Luc has to do chores. I keep him company and help him. I figure the more I can help him the faster the chores are done and then we can play. As soon as he is finished with one set of chores his mother has planned some more activities for him to do. The jobs are endless, it seems. Chores are one thing I never have to do at home.

Luc's mother is a beautiful woman. Her name is Maria and I love her. Whenever I go to his house she is kind and friendly to me. She always tells Luc:"Why can't you be more like Jackie, he is always polite?" He hates it when she does that. One day I go over and as I am about to knock on the door I can see her in the hall, through the glass in the door as she is coming down the stairs in her panties and bra. Boy that gets me excited. She notices me looking and she quickly puts on her peignoir. Luc's father is in the ship repair business. Sometimes we go to his father's office and we get to watch while they repair a ship in dry dock. Big arc welders are at work. He tells us not to look at the welders. We'll go blind if we do, he says. We get to go on the ship and look at the huge engines, below. We go on the bridge and we pretend to steer the ship. I imagine myself at sea, during a big storm trying to navigate the ship using only the instruments in front of me.

CHAPTER 34

I sing in the school choir. Madame Duschamps is the choir director. "Children, our choir sounds really good. In fact I think we should plan a school concert so that your parents can hear how wonderful you sing." I love too sing. She tells us to invite our parents and family. When I get home I tell Mom and Dad. "Will you come and hear me sing?"

"Jackie, I told you we would come, now be a good boy and do your homework." She says. The performance is next week Wednesday at 8:00pm at the school auditorium.

Wednesday rolls around and we've been rehearsing every day after school. The night of the performance, standing on stage, looking down at the audience I can't see Mom and Dad. I want so much for them to hear us sing. The concert starts and it's a wonderful performance. People give us a standing ovation at the end of the concert. We're all pretty proud of ourselves. Madame Duschamps said that we did well. When I get home Mom and Dad are sitting in the living room.

"Did you come to watch me sing?"

"No" is their reply "we forgot about the concert"

"But you promised to come"

"Oh well, we'll see you next time. Why don't you sing for us here?"

"No, it's not the same."

Mom says again"I want you to sing a song for us, if you do not sing, you won't sing with the choir anymore". I never sang with the choir again.

Madame Duschamps is also the French teacher. She is standing at the front of the class. She likes to move around, we have to watch her wherever she goes, and she talks only in French.

"Oui Madame" we respond. "Le tableau est noir" we repeat. The boy behind me, his name is Rudy Bergman. "Veffer, you're a dirty Jew." Did I hear him correctly? How does any one know that I am Jewish? It's not written on my face. "Dirty Jew" he whispers again. I turn around; I look at him for a while. Then I slap him hard across the face. Madame comes over quickly and says" Veffer, why did you do that?" I figure I'm in deep trouble, but I don't care. It felt good to take out my anger on Rudy. "Madame, he called me a dirty Jew." To my surprise, Madame nods with approval, "then you did the right thing to slap him, and he deserves it." She turns towards Rudy, whose face is beat red. She says, "I want you to apologize to Jackie, right now." Looking away from me, he softly says, "I'm sorry." Madame yells, "Louder I want to whole class to hear it." "I'm sorry, I'm sorry," he sobs. I feel neither victory nor exultation, just pity for this poor creature. I certainly did not expect this turn of events. Later, at home I tell Mom and Dad what happened at school. They too think I did a righteous thing by slapping Rudy. "Good, don't let anyone call you that and get away with it. The next time they'll think twice to call you that name."

CHAPTER 35

Dad's business is thriving. His customers, mostly Walloons, like him very much. Walloons are usually not kindly disposed to anyone except their own. They are not very tolerant of other Belgians, whether they be French or Flemish speaking. Therefore, for them to like someone who is Jewish and from Holland is quite remarkable. Dad, to his credit, treats his customers well; solicitous to their needs and always willing to please them he has generated tremendous customer loyalty. He speaks French to them, and he does this in his own unique style, with some Dutch thrown in. People laugh but they love him for trying it. Dad also has customers in Sweden and Denmark. The flowers are expedited by plane. They have to get to very fast. Once we fill the orders at home, in our big garage, that does double duty as a warehouse, we have to take them to the airport in Melsbroek, near Brussels. From there they are flown to Stockholm, Sweden or Copenhagen, Denmark. Raymond now helps Dad on a full time basis. Several enquiries for flowers come from Germany. Dad refuses to have anything to do with the Germans.

"If they were the last customers on earth and I had nothing to eat, I would never do business with the Krauts." He tells Mom.

"But Jules it's good for business. Aren't you carrying your hate a little too far?"

"Shut up woman. How dare you ask me that? After what they did to us Jews. The subject is closed." Dad has the last word and the issue is never discussed again.

Raymond is very good in the business, but dad always yells at him. He calls him a "kaffer" and makes Raymond feel bad about himself. No matter how hard he tries, Dad is never happy with his performance. Raymond drives the truck most of the time, while Dad drives his Oldsmobile. Dad leaves for Holland on Sunday nights and stays at the Hotel Schiller on the Rembrandtplein in Amsterdam, "So that I can be in Aalsmeer as soon as the auction starts on Monday," he says. Monday's and Thursday's Raymond goes and picks up the flowers in Aalsmeer and Tuesday's and Friday's they travel to the customers together.

Because he has so many customers now, it is impossible to see them all in one day, so Dad telephones some of them on the nights that he returns from Aalsmeer and takes their orders over the telephone. There are quite a number of orders to be shipped via rail. On the nights that I have no homework I help. Dad yells at me too "Hurry up, it's not your sister, they won't break, kaffer," he yells. He scares me. I don't talk to him for the rest of the night. I ask Raymond "Why is he like that?" Raymond answers "He does not mean it; he is really a nice kind person." In the next moment dad is yelling at Raymond "Hurry up, why are you so slow, we're going to miss the train. Get these orders ready now and stop wasting time talking." I feel bad for Raymond, but I'm kinda glad I'm not the one being yelled at. The orders are all packed in bog boxes and ready to go to the train station in Heide. I go with Raymond. Just as we arrive the train pulls in and we load the flowers into the freight car, with the help of the station employee. Thank goodness we made it there on time; otherwise we would have to go to Central Station in Antwerp to drop the orders off there.

There is a library in Heide. I read so much now that I go to the library on Sunday mornings and take out a bunch of books. I read adventure and mystery stories. The stories of Karl May, a German writer, he writes about the Old West, though he's never set foot in America. I particularly like mysteries written by Agatha Christie. Aunt Ninon is a French speaking Belgian so I've learned to speak and read French. I read French stories by Alexander Dumas and Victor Hugo. While at the library I pick out books for dad, he wants mostly westerns "and whatever else I think is good." he says. I pick out one book entitled "No Orchids for Miss Blandish" by James Hadley Chase. I secretly read the story. It's my first erotic novel. I rather like the feeling I get when I read it. Now I'm hungry for more erotic novels. I am afraid to read them in front of Mom and Dad, so I find a hideaway upstairs in the attic. There I discover that Mom has a library of books stashed away in boxes. When I go through them I find Emile Zola's, Nana and Germinal and the Dreyfus Affair. Zola is a good writer.

CHAPTER 36

Bram van Praag and his wife Bep are good friends of the family. They come over and visit regularly. The van Praag's live in Brussels and the visits are more or less reciprocal. They come and visit one week and the following week we'll go and visit them. Bep has impeccable taste. Her house is tastefully decorated, with exquisite antique period pieces and oriental carpets. Dad makes good-natured fun of her by reminding her that he knew her from the Jodenbuurt (Jewish Neighbourhood) in Amsterdam when she was plain Beppie Bollen with the pigtails. Her parents were very poor and made a precarious living picking up scrap metal and other junk. Bram, her husband, is a well-known tailor in demand by royalty, politicians and the rich and famous in Belgium. Dad gets his suits made there also. They cost a king's ransom, but they're "de rigueur" once you've achieved a certain social status. Bram is a simple guy, not given to airs. He treats his own fame with self-effacing detachment. The luncheons and dinners they prepare for our get-togethers are sumptuous affairs, the food being wholesome, deliciously well prepared and mercifully short, not like the endless dinner affairs at our house.

Bram is somewhat of an intellectual, very interesting to talk to and he is a welcome source of information on current affairs. His passion is Zionism, the national movement for the return of the Jewish people to their homeland and the resumption of Jewish sovereignty in the land of Israel.

***

Theodor Herzl, the one person that first envisioned the idea of Zionism, was born in Hungary in 1860. In 1894, Captain Alfred

Dreyfus, a Jewish officer in the French army, was unjustly accused of treason, mainly because of the prevailing anti-Semitic atmosphere. Herzl witnessed mobs shouting "Death to the Jews" in France, the home of the French Revolution, and resolved that there was only one solution: the mass immigration of Jews to a land that they could call their own. Thus, the Dreyfus Case became one of the determinant factors in the birth of Zionism. It was at that point that Herzl concluded that anti-Semitism was an immutable factor in human society, which assimilation did not solve. Herzl decided that anti-Semitism was not an individual problem but that it affected the entire worldwide Jewish population as a whole. He decided therefore that Jews could never gain world acceptance unless they became unified in one Jewish state, with the approval of the great powers in the world. He organized a method of attracting funds for Zionism with the single purpose of purchasing large tracts of land in Palestine for the ultimate establishment of the Jewish state of Eretz Israel. He saw the future state as a model, modern enlightened, social state. It would be a neutral peace-loving, secular state. His famous quote is "In Basle I founded the Jewish state...Maybe in five years, certainly in fifty, everyone will realize it." (The Jewish State, Theodor Hertzl).

We have just witnessed the establishment of the independent state of Israel in 1948 in a narrow vote at the United Nations. On Friday May 14, 1948 (the day in which the British Mandate over Palestine expired) the "Declaration of the Establishment of the State of Israel" was signed by members of the National Council gathered at the Tel Aviv Museum, representing the Jewish community in the country and the Zionist movement abroad. It went into effect at midnight, Tel Aviv time. Long live the State of Israel.

***

Dad has a customer Mrs. Waflard. They have a big store in Liege. They sell flowers in one section and Mr. Waflard has expensive antiques in the other section of the store. Madame Waflard is quite sick with breast cancer and she cannot tend to her business. The

Waflards owe dad a lot of money. In settlement, he chooses a massive dining room set made from rare and expensive black walnut and inlaid ivory. The set consists of an intricately carved table and eight chairs and two massive buffets. A rare Persian rug rounds out the settlement. It requires special movers to transport the dining room set to our house in Kapellenbos. Our dining room is very large and the stuff fits quite well.

Mom says "it looks simply elegant, particularly with the carpet underneath." Dad is so pleased that as a surprise he buys Mom a necklace of matched 5mm black pearls from Majorca. Dad says that thanks to the business doing so well we are now quite wealthy. The economy is booming. The reconstruction of Europe is nearly complete, hastened by the generosity of the Americans under the Marshall plan. Dad makes fun of the newly rich and calls them "Parvenus". Little does he realize that he himself is one of the new rich flaunting his wealth. Mom and Dad love to show off in quite extraordinary ways. We have these interminable dinner parties with people that we hardly know. Expensive gifts are exchanged and people generally try to outdo each other in their extravagances. Juliana, Raymond and I have to sit at the dinner table for hours while course after course is served up. There is a wait time between courses of about fifteen to thirty minutes. All the while the children are not allowed to talk. It is sheer torture and we children hate it. We don't like caviar or escargots or Paté de foie gras. We have to eat it regardless. I do like Pacific smoked salmon, the lobster, the Malpeque oysters, the tiger shrimp, and the langoustes. We don't get to drink the Chateau Neuf du Pape wine or the Lanson Brut champagne. After a while, the guests, including Mom and Dad, get quite drunk and boisterous. The children have to be quiet. We don't even get a pee break. The torture is finally finished and we are allowed to leave the table while everyone retires to the living room with a glass of cognac. I go looking for an unoccupied washroom. All of them are occupied. I nearly pee in my pants. Squeezing myself I wait until one becomes available. Then nothing comes out as hard as I might try. After what seems like an hour the pee starts to come, first a few drops, then a welcome all relieving spurt. I was worried there for a moment that my penis was broken due to the long wait. I tell Juliana the story and she laughs, she thinks it's quite funny. I am not amused.

***

The United Nations Security Council votes overwhelmingly to send troops to Korea to help resolve the conflict between the Koreans North of the 38th parallel and Korea south of the 38th parallel. This temporary partition of the country came about when Japan surrendered, after the Second World War. The Allied forces command orders Japanese commanders that were in Korea north of the 38th parallel to surrender to Soviet forces, and those that were south of the parallel to surrender to the United States forces. The United Nations, in the meantime, establishes a commission to oversee an election to be held in 1948. The Soviet Union does not allow the North to participate. Instead, the North Korean Communist Party elects Kim Il-Sung. He had spent several years in exile in Moscow, as its leader. The South Koreans elect Syngman Rhee, who spent years in exile with a Korean provisional government located in Shanghai, as speaker of the National Assembly. An armed conflict starts in 1950 between North and South Korea. Mainly American forces augmented by, among others, Belgian and Australian forces, support the South Koreans. The North Koreans get support from the Chinese and the Soviets. The war in Korea concludes with no clear winner. An uneasy armistice is negotiated. The demarcation line is the 38th parallel with a large military presence on either side to oversee the shaky truce. Many infractions are reported and both parties are forever lodging complaints to the United Nations Security Council.

***

CHAPTER 37

Dad and Mom have decided, without consultation with us kids that we will are going to the French Riviera this summer. Dad just took delivery of his midnight blue 1953 Oldsmobile Rocket 98. We're all excited because we will travel in the new car. One bright sunny morning, fully packed, we head out on our long awaited vacation. I graduated grade 8 at the top of my class. I am pleased with myself and Mom and Dad are very proud of my accomplishment. Learning comes very easy. I don't work at it. I hardly ever have any homework. Mr. Mol, My teacher, tells me that starting next year, in High school, that will all change. I will have to apply myself and do lots of homework. "No more coasting," he says. I am not worried. For now, I'll just enjoy the summer holidays. Over the years I have learned to be solicitous and attentive to the needs of Mom and Dad, professing my love for them and that I always tell them that I am thankful that they are my adoptive parents, although they cannot officially adopt me. Little do they suspect that I harbour a deep resentment for always having to act as if I love them and that since they are not really my parents, that which they give me, food and shelter, has a bittersweet taste to it. Deep inside I am still hoping that my real Mom and Dad will come to rescue me.

At times it is difficult to make sense of life, but today I just have to set it aside and enjoy the moment. We drive for hours until we cross the Belgian-France border checkpoint and we stop for lunch at a quaint little restaurant in Calais. We drive all the way to Reims after lunch and we decide to stay there overnight. We stay in a beautiful hotel right on the main street. We go for a stroll and we stop at a restaurant for supper. We are right in the middle of Champagne country; dad orders a bottle of champagne. Juliana and I have a glass each. It tastes really good, bubbly and somewhat sweet. Then he pours us a second glass. I feel strange in my head. I can't seem to concentrate very well and I am so sleepy. I am happy when we arrive back at the hotel and I can lie down. Juliana and I share a room and Mom and Dad have their own room. I fall asleep with my clothes on. We leave quite early the next morning right after breakfast, and we drive all the way to Aix-en-Provence, which is in the South of France. Pretty tired, after the long drive we go to bed after a light snack. In the washroom I look everywhere for the toilet. Can't it anywhere. I go and ask mom and dad where it is. They laugh and point at a hole in the floor. "That's where you go" Mom says. "You hold on to the rope above your head, see? Then you put a foot on one side of the hole and the other foot on the other side of the hole. Make sure you aim right." "What if I have to poo," I ask. "Same idea" she says"but aim better. You don't want to have to clean up after you've missed the hole." I can't believe how weird this is. "Why can't they have regular toilets?" Non-plussed I shake my head. "Juliana, how do women go on these toilets? They don't have the same equipment as men do? "They squat over the hole silly, "she says. The washroom also has a bidet. This is the first time I've seen a bidet. "What is it for Juliana?" I ask. She says "for a woman to clean her parts afterwards down there" and she points at herself. This has sure been an educational day.

The next day we drive all the way to Nice. We have to cross the Pyrenees first. We drive up the mountain. There is no barrier most of the way. I'm afraid that we'll go over the edge. Dad is a good driver thank goodness. When we reach the top travel down on the other side. I can see the Mediterranean from there. It's a spectacular sight. When we reach Nice, we drive down the Promenade Des Anglais and we stop at the Negresco Hotel where we will be staying. The hotel is on one side of the Promenade and the sandy beach and the sea is on the other side. The promenade is crowded. Thousands of people are walking. We can't wait to go and swim. The porter unloads the car and we all go to our rooms first, unpack, put on our bathing suits and then we can go swimming. We have a bit of lunch first and Mom informs that now we have to wait three hours before we can go in the water, otherwise we'll get cramps and drown in the ocean. Thanks a lot Mom, "Why didn't you tell us before we ate. So we sit on the beach in a chaise lounge waiting for three hours to pass. I cast sideways glances at the beautiful women that lay topless, their breasts glistening in the sunlight. I feel strange stirrings in my stomach. I don't want mom and dad to see me looking at these women. I can't help looking at them.

Juliana sees me looking and she asks," Do you like what you see?"

"What are you talking about?" angry that I got found out.

"You know what I mean, I see you looking at the women." Why does she always make fun of me? Boy I hate her.

After the compulsory three hour wait we can go in the water now. It's none too soon. The water is warm and the sea, in perpetual motion, is calm. Little whitecaps roll over on to the sand and spill their content gently into a puddle that started because the tide is rising. It feels like nothing matters the world has come to a standstill. There is hardly any wind. I start walking into the sea caught up in the stillness of the day, alone with my thoughts, what seems for miles and the water is still only up to my knees.

Mom yells after me, cupping her hands around her mouth, "Did you apply Bain de Soleil?"

"Oh, Mom, the sun is setting; it's late in the day. I won't get sunburned."

"Suit yourself it's your body. Don't come crying to me when the sun burns you." Mothers always make you feel guilty about something. The implied threat almost makes me come back to put on the stupid sunscreen. Ah, the heck with it. It'll be OK, besides I am so far in now I don't want to waste any more precious moments. She should have told me before I went in. It's her fault if I get burnt.

I am self-conscious about the burn scars on my chest and my arm. It looks awful, all puffy and red. I don't like taking my shirt off because people always stare at me. They want to know how I got burned and I don't feel like telling them. I don't want to talk about it.

We spend lazy days in the sun, sun bathing, swimming and reading books and my favourite pastime, looking at the girls and their beautiful breasts. Juliana and I rent bikes and ride up and down the Promenade des Anglais. One day we rent pedal boats and race each other. We get tired and spend the rest of the time bobbing up and down on the waves pedaling from time to time so that we stay within easy reach of the shore, just in case a freak storm comes up. You never know, it could happen.

Dad announces that we are driving down the coast towards the Italian Riviera. We drive to San Remo. As luck will have it we arrive during the Italian Song festival. The first San Remo Song Festival was held in 1951. The festival was broadcast on the radio and there were only three singers competing. The following year, the number of competing singers rose to five and then to ten in 1953. The Festival is very popular now and gained prestige on the international stage and the introduction of television in 1955 was pivotal in its increased fame. Dad gets tickets for us to attend the final song competition. The shows are glamorous, glitzy affairs. Although the musical shows are all in Italian and therefore hard to understand, I have a wonderful time nevertheless. Great Italian singers and songwriters, such as Nilla Pizza, Teddy Reno, Claudio Villa, and Domenico Modugno are showcasing their latest songs. Domenico Modugno won the Festival in 1958 with his world- famous hit song "Nel blu dipinto di blu" also called Volare. San Remo is a great city. I have never seen so many beautiful women in one place before. After leaving San Remo we drive to Alasio, a beach resort town. It's not nearly as nice as the French Riviera and the smell almost makes me sick to my stomach. Thank goodness we don't stay there long. We head back towards France. We go to Monaco. Dad tells me that it is its own country, a Principality; People that live in Monaco don't pay taxes. All the tax revenue raised comes from money that people lose while gambling at the Casino in Monte Carlo. We stay in Monte Carlo for a few days at the Carlton across from the casino. One night we watch a movie in an open-air theatre. Another night we go and see a show at the Café de Paris. Our summer vacation ends far too soon. We start the long drive back to Belgium.

We were away for three weeks and while we were gone Raymond was left behind to look after the flower business. He went to pick up the flowers at the auction in Aalsmeer twice a week; he also went to visit the customers twice a week. Dad said he did very well on his own. For once he pays Raymond a compliment; he is quite pleased with himself. I run over to see Luc at his house. I can't wait to tell about all the beautiful girls I've seen and how they walked around topless. He won't believe me, I bet.

Sure enough he says,"You're just making it up to make me jealous"

"I'm not making it up; just ask Juliana, she'll confirm it." Luc doesn't believe me. We walk home and he asks Juliana "Did girls walk around showing their tits on the beach?"

"Yes, and Jackie could not keep his eyes off them." She replies in a mocking tone.

"See, I told you so," I yell in triumph. This time I love Juliana and I even ignore her making fun of me. Luc is really upset.

He keeps asking, "Well, what did they look like, exactly?"

"Some were small, and some were bigger, with big nipples" I say. At this he punches me in frustration.

"Aw man, I wish I could have been there to see it." I savour the moment because I've seen something he obviously hasn't and would love to have seen, at the same time secretly wishing I could take a peak at his mother's breasts.

CHAPTER 38

On June 2nd 1953 at 11am Greenwich meantime all across Europe people settle down in front of their television sets to watch the Coronation of Princess Elizabeth II. TV programmes usually start at eight pm, but today they begin extra early. Most people in Europe love their Royal families, and follow the lives of the royals with avid interest. I am one of those that loves the pomp and circumstance of the royal traditions and though we don't have a television of our own yet, the Kiekens have invited me to watch the coronation at their house.

The princess arrives at Westminster Abbey looking radiant, but there is a problem with the carpet in the Abbey. It has been laid with the carpet pile running the wrong way, which means that the queen's robes have trouble gliding over the carpet pile. The metal fringe on the queen's golden mantel catches in the pile of the carpet, and claws her back. It is an awkward moment. The 'Crowning Ceremony' takes place and when St. Edward's Crown is placed on the princess' head she officially becomes Elizabeth Regina, Queen of the British Realm, Her Majesty Queen Elizabeth II (Elizabeth Alexandra Mary Windsor) and head of state of Antigua and Barbuda, Australia, the Bahamas, Barbados, Belize, Canada, Grenada, Jamaica, New Zealand, Papua New Guinea, Saint Kitts and Nevis, Saint Lucia, Saint Vincent and the Grenadines, the Solomon Islands, Tuvalu and the United Kingdom of Great Britain and Northern Ireland. She is also Head of the Commonwealth, Supreme Governor of the Church of England, Commander-in-Chief of the UK Armed Forces and Lord of Mann;

So, in spite of the rain, the Coronation of Queen Elizabeth II is a day to remember. 'God save the Queen'.

The war in Indochina has captured my interest and I follow every detail from the daily newspaper reports. After the end of World War II, France reinstates its colonial government in Indochina. In 1946 a Vietnamese independence movement, led by communist leader Ho Chi Minh, is fighting French troops for control of northern Vietnam. The Viet Minh, as the insurgents are called, use guerrilla tactics that the French find impossible to counter. In late 1953, as both sides prepare for peace talks in the Indochina War, French military commanders pick Dien Bien Phu, a village in northwestern Vietnam near the Laotian and Chinese borders, as the place to pick a fight with the Viet Minh. Hoping to draw Ho Chi Minh's guerrillas into a classic battle, the French begin to build up their garrison at Dien Bien Phu. The stronghold is located at the bottom of a bowl-shaped river valley, about 10 miles long. Most French troops and supplies enter Dien Bien Phu from the air, either landing at the fort's airstrip or dropping in via parachute. Dien Bien Phu's main garrison is also supported by a series of firebases. These are strong points on nearby hills that rain down fire on an attacker. The strong points are given women's names, supposedly after the mistresses of the French commander, Gen. Christian de Castries. The French assume any assaults on their fortified positions will fail or be broken up by their artillery. The size of the French garrison at Dien Bien Phu swells to somewhere between 13,000 and 16,000 troops by March 1954. About 70 percent of that force is made up of members of the French Foreign Legion, soldiers from French colonies in North Africa, and loyal Vietnamese. Ho Chi Minh, the brilliant strategist that he is, has a battle plan of his own. Viet Minh guerrillas and troops from the People's Army of Vietnam surround Dien Bien Phu during the buildup within the French garrison. The Viet Minh assault on March 13 proves immediately how vulnerable and flawed the French defenses are. Dien Bien Phu's outlying firebases are overrun within days of the initial assault. And the main part of the garrison is amazed to find itself under heavy, artillery fire from the surrounding hills. In a major logistical feat, the Viet Minh have dragged scores of pieces of artillery up steeply forested hillsides that the French thought was impossible to accomplish. The French artillery commander, distraught at his inability to bring counter fire on the well-defended and well-camouflaged Viet Minh batteries, goes into his dugout and kills himself. Closed off from the outside world, under constant fire, and flooded by monsoon rains, conditions inside Dien Bien Phu become inhuman. Casualties pile up inside the garrison's hospital. Dien Bien Phu falls to the Viet Minh on May 7. At least 2,200 members of the French forces die during the siege—with thousands more taken prisoner. Of the 50,000 or so Vietnamese who laid siege to the garrison, there were about 23,000 casualties, including an estimated 8,000 killed. The fall of Dien Bien Phu shocks France and brings an abrupt end to French Indochina. I am absolutely amazed at the brilliant tactics and the complete and swift victory of the Viet Minh. It played out like a chess game.

CHAPTER 39

Since the end of the war, school boards in Belgium have instituted medical examinations for all the students. Teams of doctors and nurses visit all schools once a year. This is one of life's embarrassing moments, I find. All male students gather in one section of the school on the designated day. Girls have their examinations on a different day. We all have to strip down to our underwear and stand around for what seems like hours. We get called into the room where the medical examinations take place one at a time. Finally it is my turn to go in for the examination. The doctor holds a stethoscope to my chest and back, asks me to breathe deeply and cough. Then he pulls down my underpants, checks around my testicles and asks me to cough again. I swear the nurse is laughing at me. I'm afraid I'll get an erection in front of her. I would be so ashamed if that happened and I fret about it all day. The doctor mumbles something unintelligible to the nurse. She is busy writing down what he dictates. "Circumcised. Are you Jewish my boy?" he asks in a pleasant tone.

"Yes doctor." I am so embarrassed. The nurse nods with an air of approval. I guess she must like circumcised penises. With the examination over I can pull up my briefs. I am relieved that I did not get an erection. I bet she must really enjoy her job, looking at dicks all day.

Nurses visit schools to do scratch tests to see who tests positive for tuberculosis. Since I was in contact with Mom when she had TB. I always test positive. I don't get sick from it anymore. My arm swells up a little around the scratches and turns red.

I am in high school, now, at the athenaeum, in grade 9. My main interest is no longer my studies, but girls. My grades are slipping badly. I don't do any homework. My teachers voice their concern to Mom.

"Jackie, what is happening? You were always so good in school. You need to concentrate more. I will work with you and check your homework every night and I will quiz you on your subjects before a test." She works with me for a few weeks and then I am allowed to fall back into my old pattern my grades go up. I still get by on the barest minimum of effort.

One night, when Juliana is in the bathroom I peak through the keyhole to try to catch a glimpse of her in the nude. All of a sudden another eye on the other side of the door is looking back at me. I've been found out.

Juliana screams, "You filthy pig, I'm going to tell mom. Boy are you in trouble."

"Please don't tell mom, I won't do it anymore." I beg. She tells mom. I get called to the living room and I have to sit down and take my punishment. I can't imagine what the punishment could be for sneaking a peak at your sister getting undressed. Do they cut off your testicles or your penis? I sit there feeling sorry for myself, thinking the worst.

Mom says, "You really disappoint me. I never thought you of all people would do something so low and dirty." I feel terrible, not necessarily for what I did, but for being found out. I have to listen to the harangue for the next hour or so. I feign repentance. My punishment is that I have to apologize to Juliana. She comes downstairs and contritely I apologize to her in a contrite voice. Without Mom being able to see her reaction, she sticks out her tongue at me. Boy, do I ever hate her.

It is February 1953 and Holland faces one of the greatest disasters in its history when the dikes protecting the southwest of the country are breached by the combination of a hurricane-force northwesterly wind and very high spring tides. The flood comes during the night without warning, a freak combination of high tides and gale-force winds that in the end kills 1,835 people. Almost 200,000 hectares of land is flooded, 3,000 homes and 300 farms are destroyed, and 47,000 heads of cattle drown. Flooding caused by storms were nothing new to the Netherlands, but this time the nation is surprised by the extent of a disaster unparalleled for centuries. It was The Netherlands' worst disaster for 300 years. Emergency aid flowed in from all over the world to help soften the blow to a country only just recovering from war. Juliana and I are moved to go to all the villas in the area in Kapellenbos and canvas for clothes and bedding, whatever people can spare. Everybody responds with so much that we can barely store it in our large garage. Not only do we sort it all in neat piles we also organize transportation and pick up of all the goods to a central point where everything is gathered for shipment to the stricken areas. Ironically enough, the Ministry of Transport, Public Works and Water Management had published a policy document only a few days' earlier outlining plans to prevent precisely this sort of disaster. The document proposed that all the tidal inlets and estuaries in the provinces of Zeeland and South Holland should be dammed. In the light of the disaster, urgent action was taken to implement this plan, known as the 'Delta Project'.

My biggest fear in life is that I have cancer. Any type of cancer scares me. I check myself on a daily basis for lumps and bumps. This morning I wake up and I feel two lumps, one on either side of my Adams apple. Immediately I think the worst. Cancer of the throat is what I have. I've only got a little while to live. I tell no one, scared that my deepest fears will be confirmed. I develop a sore throat. Mom takes me to Dr. van den Heuvel. He checks the lumps in my throat,

He says, "You got swollen glands and a strepped throat."

"I don't have cancer?"

"No, not this time." The doctor laughs. I don't think it's very funny. However, I am relieved. The next day I feel a lump at the top of my thigh in the crease near my scrotum. Afraid that I will lose my leg to cancer, I suffer in silence.

Sitting in class during French, one day, I find it hard to swallow again, and immediately my concern about having cancer increases my temperature. Sweating now and hyper ventilating the teacher addresses me:"Veffer, qu'est ce qui a? Tu es malade?" I'm definitely not feeling well at this point. The teacher instructs Louis Vingerhoedt, who sits next to me, to take me to the school infirmary. The nurse takes one look at me and places a brown paper bag over my head. She tells me to take shorter breaths of air. My breathing returns to normal and my anxiety subsides.

"You got to stop doing this to yourself." She says,"Remember every time, when you get an anxiety attack try to slow down and think happy thoughts, don't think you're going to die every time." I swallow hard a couple times and I can feel my Adams apple dislocating. The pain is instant and intense. Panicked I point at my throat and the nurse grabs my Adams apple and gives it a push to the left and thank God I can feel it snap back into position. Luckily this happened while I was in competent hands. I'm thinking what would have happened if the nurse was not around to do what she did for me? What a scary thought.

CHAPTER 40

Raymond has a girlfriend, Freda. I met her; she lives down the road in a villa with her grandmother. She is very pretty and a few years older than Raymond. He loves her very much.

One day Raymond says, "I can make oil come out of my penis."

"Go away with you, that's impossible." I answer

"Do you want to see? I don't really want to see it, but he insists. He starts pulling at his penis and after a while he starts to breathe as if he is in pain. Suddenly white squirts of oil come out of his penis. I am amazed. "You want me to do it to you" he asks.

Horrified I say, "No, thank you."

"It feels really good, you'll like it, I promise." Intrigued I give in. Nothing happens.

"You have to think of naked women." Raymond urges. I think of Luc's mother naked. After an hour of Raymond massaging my penis, suddenly I feel the most indescribable pleasurable feeling coming up from the depth of my being. Then my penis starts to squirt. I can barely catch my breath. The feeling is so intense that I can hardly stand it. I lay there not wanting the pleasure to end. The feeling subsides and now I am really embarrassed. A sense of shame comes over me and I try to forget about what just happened. Raymond won't let me. The next day he says that I have to do it to him. After his pleading I give in. It takes only a few moments for him. Relieved that it is over I can now go to sleep. Every so often he asks me to do it for him and I give in every time. One day he says that Freda sticks his penis in her mouth and would I do that for him.

Horrified I answer, "Are you nuts? I would never, ever do that." I say with disgust in my voice. He does not pursue the matter further.

I start to masturbate daily, sometimes two or three times a day. It becomes an obsession. That's all I can think about.

Dad finds out that Raymond has a girlfriend.

"Freda is too old for you and she is a fortune hunter and after our money. I forbid you to see her again." He says in his most threatening voice. Despite the threat Raymond continues to see her in secret, of course.

"Dad can't stop me. I'm 19 and I can do what I want." Dad catches him and Freda together one day and starts to beat him up. It's horrible. Dad grabs a knife and attacks Raymond. He cuts him. Blood splatters on the walls. As Dad wants to stab Raymond, Mom screams and grabs his arm. She pleads with him to let go. I have never seen such anger and hatred. Juliana and I are watching in a state of shock, not knowing what to do. It is really very scary. Raymond breaks his grip and manages to escape. He runs out the door in his stocking feet. He goes to the police station and lays an assault charge against Dad. The police come and they take Dad into custody. Thank God Raymond is not badly hurt. After getting a few stitches in his arm he is released from the hospital. He does not ever come back home to live and moves in with Freda and her grandmother. Dad is released on his own recognizance after he promises to appear in court on the assault charge. We all knew that Dad had a violent temper because he had vented it on all of us in the past. I did not think, however, that he would be capable of killing someone in cold blood. During the trial Dad pleads extreme provocation as his defense. The judge believes him and dismisses the case. I resolve in my mind that I must get away from this madman at the first possible opportunity.

Raymond moves to Brussels and marries Freda. They open up a flower store and do very well. But Raymond has a gambling problem. He gambles away all their money and falls in with the wrong crowd and is selling drugs. He and Freda have three children.

One day the sad news reaches us that Raymond has committed suicide by shooting himself in the head. We are all grief stricken. I loved Raymond. He was sadly misunderstood. I understood him because he shared many secret things with me. I feel privileged to have known him, and I have a sense that he looks after me from heaven. I think that Dad hated him because Raymond was not his natural son. He was talented and never got his proper due in his all too short life. He was only 24.

CHAPTER 41

I love one girl at school, I send her love letters. Her name is Eva Maas. She is the love of my life and I can't get her out of my mind. Mom finds some of the letters and reads them aloud to the family. She makes fun of me. She is not very sensitive of my feelings and I hate her for that. After all it's pretty serious business to be in love. I finish up the year at the athenaeum not having done too badly, even after goofing off the whole year.

Mom and Dad decide that a change of venue is in order. Maybe they think that I will forget about girls if they send us to private school in Antwerp. They enroll Juliana at the College Marie-Josée, a school for girls. They enroll me at the Lycée D'Anvers, an all boy's school in the Nervier Straat, right across from the Astrid Bad, the swimming pool where we learned to swim. The schools are related in that the same Board of Governors runs them. The Lycée has many kids from very rich parents. Many of them are Jewish. The Jewish kid's parents are mostly in the Diamond industry located in the Pelikaan Straat, not far from where the Lycée is. Many other boys also attend the school, such as sons of diplomats and politicians and boys from parents that have been transferred to Belgium from American and other foreign firms. We are all a pretty privileged bunch to be attending this school. The one main difference with the Lycée and the Athenaeum in Kapellen is that the Lycée teaches in French and the athenaeum is a Flemish school. Although I speak French, it will be quite an adjustment to receive my education in French from now on. Luc is also in a private school in Antwerp. His school is a private catholic school. The first few mornings Dad drives us from Kapellenbos to school in Antwerp. It takes approximately 45 minutes. Not long after he decides that it will be more convenient for us to take the train each morning. School starts at eight o'clock. Therefore we have to be at the train station to leave Kapellenbos at seven AM. Monday through Saturday. We get up at six each morning. We arrive back at about seven each night. There is no girl distraction. Learning is pretty easy for me. We do have a lot of homework, usually about two hours a day. By the time I get to bed it is about midnight. Instead of taking Belgian literature we take French literature. We learn about the works of 17th Century French writer's, Racine, Boileau, La Fontaine and Moliere. I particularly like Moliere's "Le Malade Imaginaire, Tartuffe and Misanthrope." The poetry of Jean de La Fontaine is fascinating as it uses animals to depict the human condition.

I am singled out for my impeccable use of the Flemish language during Flemish class. I speak "Algemeen Beschaafd Nederlands". That is Flemish spoken correctly. For some reason few have the ability to use the language as well as I do. They all throw in colloquialisms. I don't know why that is. Since the Lycée is a French school, I am always asked to pronounce certain Flemish words correctly. I am flattered that they ask me to do this. I am in Grade 10. The Grade 13 class is rehearsing a Flemish play. The drama teacher is looking for someone with impeccable Flemish to cast in the male lead role. He invites me to try out for the part. I am very flattered of course, and cast opposite the female heroine, Carole Gosselin. Carole is beautiful and smart. It is rather intimating for a boy like me with raging hormones. We have to do a close up scene, where we stand body to body and we have to kiss. I get a noticeable erection and am very embarrassed, especially since we will have to appear in tights. All the other boys see it and poke fun at me. The teacher seeing my embarrassment says, "That won't be a problem Mr. Veffer," pointing at my crotch, "you'll be wearing a cup. After the audition the teacher comments that I am perfect for the role and we start rehearsing right away. They give me a book with all the actor's lines.

"You memorize your lines starting tonight, Mr. Veffer."

Every day I am excused from my classes at 3pm to go to rehearsals. I am rather proud to be singled out like that in front of my peers. We spend about two months rehearsing the play. I've memorized all my lines after the first week. We have two rehearsals at the KNS, Koningkle Nederlandse Schouwburg, (Royal Dutch Theater) in Antwerp. The first one is to get us used to the difference in acoustics.

The second one is the dress rehearsal, one night before the performance. I feel strange and self-conscious in my tights. Francisco Fandino, one of my friends, teases me about my prominent crotch. I tell him that the cup makes it look even bigger.

Mom and Dad get notification way in advance that I will be performing in the lead role. They promise me, that this time, they will come and watch me. They will not miss it for the world. Performance night is a jittery, nerve-wracking time. Hours before the performance my stomach starts to hurt. It is so painful that I am doubled up in pain. I don't think I can perform. The drama teacher is concerned; he assures me that come curtain time the pain will subside. He gives me deep breathing exercises to do, and he tells me to lay down for a while in the dressing room. I start to feel a little better, my stomach still hurts, but I think I can go on now. The curtain rises sharply at 8pm. We have a full house for the performance. Everything goes very well. I have not forgotten any of my lines. We have the added security of a prompter in the stage floor. During the performance I attempt to scan the audience to locate Mom and Dad. It's impossible to see anyone in the audience because the stage is lit up and the hall is in almost total darkness. The play ends and the audience gives us a standing ovation. Each performer takes a bow and when I come out for my bow the applause volume really increases. I am so very proud. The house lights are on. I can't see Mom and Dad anywhere. The parents of all the other actors come on stage after the performance. Mine are nowhere to be seen. I am so terribly disappointed. I have to take the train home and on the way I feel sorry for myself. I bemoan the fact that there is no one in this whole wide world with whom I can share my triumphs or commiserate about my misfortunes. No one bears witness to my life. If life is worth living, someone needs to be there to share it with you. My brother is in Canada leading his own life. Where are my real father and mother? I am sure they would have come to watch me. Who is an observer to my life? How can I be validated and gain a sense of self worth. All my young life I've had to live by my own wits. To be sure I've learned the system to get me what I want. What I am unable to attain is a sense of being part of something. Feeling all alone, it has never mattered before, until tonight. On the train, alone with my thoughts, I realize that even the most triumphant fulfilling experience, matters not unless you can share it with someone. Someone that says to you "Atta boy, job well done." When I get home I them why they did not come. "Sorry, we forgot" is their lame reply. I go straight to bed without saying goodnight. I cry tears of frustration.

My love for reading is what keeps me sane, devouring at least two books a week. Recently I have started to read more books written by Karl May. The author was born in 1842 and died in 1912. He was a prolific writer and a favourite read of many famous Germans, including Albert Einstein, Albert Schweitzer, and Herman Hesse. According to the Karl May Press based in Bamberg, his works have sold over 100 million copies across the globe, and his 60 novels have been translated into over 30 languages, including a recent series in Chinese. The books I love the most were his best-known works, Winnetou, published in three volumes. The story depicts the friendship of Old Shatterhand, an American pioneer of German descent, and Winnetou, the noble Red Indian chief, "roten Gentleman" (the Red Gentleman). Before his death in the third book, Winnetou abandons his Indian gods and accepts Christianity. All the stories were concocted in his fertile mind despite the fact that he never set foot in the United States.

On Saturdays we go to school a half a day and because Dad takes the day off he drives me to school, from time to time. He drops me off right in front of the big school doors in his new Oldsmobile. Students congregate outside and watch what goes on. Some are smoking, although it's forbidden by the school authorities. It's the in-cool thing to do. Imitators, not innovators, we parrot the super-cool of the silver screen, Humphrey Bogart, Lauren Bacall, Eddy Constantine and George Simenon's Inspecteur Maigret, as played by the coolest Jean Gabin. Smoking and drinking coffee, and wearing black turtleneck sweaters makes us feel as if we invented Sartre's existentialism, his famous work "L'Existentialisme est un humanisme" being required reading. Not that we understand any of it, mind you. Image is everything and of course we would never want to shatter that image in front of our friends, do we? Dad insists that I give him a kiss when I exit from the car. There is no way it can be done in a nonchalant manner. So right there in full super panoramic view I have to plant a wet one on Dad's invited cheek. Talk about an image buster. I hate him. My friends tease me about it, of course. I wish I could die.

Francisco Fandino is my best friend. His father is the Consul General from Columbia. They live only minutes from where the Lycée is located on the Belgielei. At lunchtime I go to Francisco's house for something to eat. Other times we'll go across the street to the Astrid bad to watch the girls swim while we have our lunch. We can overlook the swimming pool from the glassed in restaurant. Every so often the girls from the College Marie-Josée come and join us. We play foosball with them. The girls like Francisco; he is quite a lady's man. That is what I like about him. I am clumsy around girls. It's as if I just developed two left feet and where did the stutter come from all of a sudden?

"You respect girls too much." Francisco says. "The worst you treat them the better they like it."

"Show me how." I trust his judgment, because he's had a lot more experience with them than I have. He's been all over the world because his dad is a diplomat.

"Just watch me and learn my boy. Have you taken a girl to bed yet?

"No", I reply. Although I wish I had.

"I've been to bed with plenty of them." He brags. I am really envious of him. Mom and dad disapprove of our friendship.

Dad warns me, "I forbid you to see him. He can teach you no

good." Although I am always obedient, this time my resolve is not to give up my friendship with Francisco. There is so much I can learn from him. I make an excuse to stay in Antwerp instead of going home straight away, after school. I do this on a regular basis. Francisco and I, as well as other friends go to a café close to the Lycée. We drink Trappist beer, a nice smooth dark beer, brewed by the Trappist monks for centuries. Most times the girls from the college Marie-Josée come and join us. We have a great time. Francisco and his girlfriend always smooch. I am too shy to get involved with any of the girls, even though I would dearly love to. Because of my theater performance I am somewhat of a hero. I like being in the limelight. We listen to music from the jukebox and watch the foot traffic go by on the Keyserlei. Rock and Roll is all the rage. Music by Bill Hailey and his Comets, Rock around the clock, is currently number one. The Platters' The Great Pretender is right up on the charts too. We put on music from the Four Diamonds so it gives us a chance to dance close with the girls. Paul Anka singing Diana is a heavy favourite, as is Harry Belafonte's song, something about picking bananas. The song scene is a mixed bag at the moment. We still have crooners like Frank Sinatra, Vic Damone, Dean Martin and Eddie Fisher, but it is pretty clear that Rock and Roll is here to stay and is hugely popular with us teenagers. We, after all are the ones that buy the most records. As is custom all of us follow the Hollywood scene up close. We know what's going on with the stars from the magazines. I am pretty angry with Vic Damone for leaving his wife Pier Angeli, but happy that Bobby Darin and Sandra Dee are getting along so well. These issues are of great importance to us these days, existentialism be damned. Hollywood is so much larger than life; it makes the rest of us happy when exciting things befall our heroes and heroines. The film festival at Cannes is a highlight for the movie going public and for a few weeks once a year everyone watches the glitz and glamour and the slight excesses with good-natured humour. Brigitte Bardot an up and coming actress is strutting her stuff for the paparazzi. She just finished a movie directed by her husband; director Roger Vadim called "Et Dieu Créa la Femme" (God Created Woman). The French go crazy for Brigitte Bardot and so does the rest of the European movie going public. She's got the perkiest little titties and doesn't mind showing them. What I wouldn't give for an evening out with Brigitte. During the festival Prince Rainier of Monaco meets Grace Kelly. After, they are rumoured to be romantically involved. This is a true-life fairy story that causes great excitement. Sure enough they announce their wedding plans to the world and the whole world stops for a brief moment to watch the Royal wedding in Monaco.

CHAPTER 42

A new family just moved into our neighbourhood. Because it is a small close knit community made up of mostly affluent families, this is a rare, much discussed, occasion. Who are these people? Where do they come from? Do they have money? These are the "de rigueur" questions. We find out that they are the Dodge family from Paterson, New Jersey. The American firm mister Dodge works for Continental Can Company transferred him, to manage the Belgian subsidiary just outside of Antwerp. They have three kids, Merton the eldest son is my age. Liz his sister is a few years younger and little Joey, he is eight years old. They are a colourful lot according to Belgian standards. The whole family wears Levy blue jeans, a somewhat novel item of apparel in Europe. Blue jeans don't have buttons; they have something called a zipper, a very clever invention indeed. When Liz wears skirts, which is not often, they are a multicoloured, wide flowing affair, with a crinoline underneath the skirt to make the whole thing stand out. To finish the look she wears "Bobby socks", white socks, and as footwear she sports sneakers. Her hair is always done up in what she calls a "pony tail". Merton also wears white socks and sneakers. As a shirt he wears something called a Tee Shirt, a white undershirt with short sleeves. When at home relaxing, he wears his jeans and only a tee shirt without a regular shirt over top. This is a little different than what we are used to. I would never be allowed to show myself in only my undershirt. It's just not done in our family. Little Joey is a mini-version of Merton. Merton is enrolled at the Lycée and Liz at the college Marie-Josée. Due to the fact that they attend the same schools as Juliana and me, we are invited over to their house quite often. Mom and Dad, being vocal of their barbaric ways, have no intention of reciprocating. They don't really know what to make of these Americans and their strange ways. I like American food. They eat potato chips; these are thinly sliced, deep-fried potatoes. They are crunchy, very tasty and quite addictive. This is the first time Juliana and me experience this unique tasting product. Mrs. Dodge explains that chips have been around for a long time in America, but are only now being introduced into the European market. Mr. Dodge also Barbeques food on an open fire. Things called Hot Dogs are not really heated up dogs, they are sausages eaten with mustard and relish and sauerkraut or beans on a special long bun, quite delicious. I can eat several. For the first time in our lives Juliana and I have the pleasure of eating a hamburger. Hamburgers don't have an ounce of ham in them. It is ground meat burnt to a crisp on the ubiquitous barbeque and placed between two slices of a round soft bun, appropriately named a hamburger bun. Sometimes as an added touch it is served with a slice of cheddar cheese that melts into the hamburger. My Jewish forefathers are surely turning over in their graves by now. All of this is washed down with large quantities of Coca Cola. They have a large supply of this drink cooled and waiting to be consumed in the refrigerator. If they aren't drink coke (Coca Cola) they drink milk and I am in awe of the amount of milk they consume in a day. No wonder Americans are big people. Americans blow their noses in paper handkerchiefs called Kleenex. We always use a cloth handkerchief. Are Kleenex handkerchiefs not porous, I wonder? Where do they wipe their hands after they have blown their noses? Maybe another Kleenex. We find the whole thing a bit unsanitary. The neat thing about the Dodge's is there easygoing ways, making everyone feel comfortable. We love going there; Juliana and I, and we realize how different the family is towards one another compared to our own relationship with our parents. At night the whole Dodge family plays games like Monopoly or card games like Pinochle. They also love outdoor games. Since they have a very large backyard, they play a number of games that we have never seen in Belgium. Baseball and Football. Merton ties to teach me the rudimentary rules of both games. As much as I try to understand the basics of three downs, the object of the game eludes me. The same goes for baseball with three strikes and you're out, is something I cannot quite grasp. Part of the difficulty is that I don't speak English and therefore the language makes no sense, particularly if we don't even understand the object and technicalities of the games. We watch and so we learn. The entire Dodge family gets involved, including Mrs. Dodge. It's too funny to watch them tackle each other. We never play games at home.

Merton, even tough he is only 15 is allowed to drive his dad's new 1955 Ford Fairlane station wagon in Belgium. No driver's license is required here. They brought their car from the U.S.A. The colour, instead of being black like all American cars here, is a two tone green. I have never seen a station wagon until now. Merton and I go riding late at night on deserted roads. He guns the car. Tires spinning and squealing, we take off in a cloud of black smoke. Merton explains that in the States, as he calls it, usually two cars will take off simultaneously racing each other. He boasts that he has been involved in a few road races like that, though it is illegal for him to drive in the States at age 15. We drive around to see if we can pick up girls. In Kapellenbos where we live, unfortunately, at ten o'clock at night there is no one on the street, let alone girls walking by themselves. We are not allowed to go Antwerp in the car either.

Juliana falls in love with Merton. That is all she talks about. Merton this and Merton that. She only thinks of him. He is not the least bit interested in her. It is affecting her every day life. Her grades drop, she is driving herself crazy. I'm afraid she will get sick if she keeps this up. And then one day, as suddenly as her love for him started, it ends, without warning and it's a good thing to, because being so badly smitten can't be good for you. Maybe it has something to do with unrequited love.

Mr. Dodge, since he is driving Merton and Liz anyway, has offered to drive us to school daily and bring us back home at night. This saves a lot of time. It means that I can sleep in an extra thirty minutes in the morning and at night instead of coming at 7:30pm we get home at 6:30pm.This is a very kind offer but Mom and Dad still don't extend an invitation to the Dodge's. It's kind of embarrassing to Juliana and me because we are over at their place so many times. They don't mind however. We realize that Americans are very generous, good natured, kind people. They do care about what other people think of them.

The Lycée is arranging a vacation for the students at an International Holiday camp, Colomendy, in North Wales, near a tiny village called Mold. Liverpool is not that far away. I really want to go. Mom and Dad want to go to the South of France again. They want Juliana and I join them. I don't really want to go with them.

"I would much rather go to Colomendy with my friends."

"You're an ingrate" she says. Maybe, but I'd rather go with my friends and do the things I enjoy doing, instead of going with them and always having to do what they want to do. She does not understand that and I think she is a stupid cow. What does she know about me anyway? I have to be able to lead my own life. I feel great hostility towards them. They won't let me do anything on my own. If I want to go to the city on my own to see my friends, they say I am not allowed. If I want to go out at night they say I am too young to go. They won't allow me to do anything except go to school and return. All my friends are allowed to go out at night, why can't I? I am at the age where I need to be able to experience the things that other teenagers are experiencing. This includes going out on dates and learning stuff that my friends are learning. I think it is a right of passage. As time goes on my movements are being more and more restricted under the pretext that they are looking after my best interest. They insist that they know much better than I about what is good for me. I would rather experience things for myself, thank you very much. I think it is OK to venture out and make mistakes and thereby learn life's valuable lessons. Mom figures, from my body language, that I am not happy with the way they are trying to control my life. Never really having been confrontational I sulk and protest against their narrow-minded ways, in silence. I go quiet and won't speak to them for days on end. It irritates them and they threaten me with severe punishment if I keep up the silent treatment. As much as I want to communicate with them it is impossible for me to engage in conversation. They interpret this as stubbornness on my part. They can't find anything to punish me with, simply because they won't let me do anything on my own anyway. So they take away my reading privileges. I can't read any books for the next month. Reading is the only form of escape I have left and they manage to take that away from me too. Talk about being petty. This takes the cake in the annals of vindictive. My resentment towards them deepens. I sulk for weeks. One day Mom says that they discussed it and that if I still want to go to Colomendy, they would let me go, even though they think it is wrong and I should go with them. She says that they realize I am getting older now and that I want to spend time with my friends. This is a major concession on their part. There is hope for them yet, I conclude. Excited I tell Francisco that I can go. He is happy also. There are quite a few of us going from the Lycée and about ten girls from the college are also going. The trip is still two months away. I realize that it is the trip of a lifetime; it will be fun being with my friends for a whole month.

CHAPTER 43

It's been my secret wish to become a teacher, ever since the fifth grade. While attending the fifth grade at the athenaeum I had a wonderful teacher, Mr. Rommel was his name. I loved him because he managed to bring alive anything that he taught the kids. He had a special way of instructing. You could envision it in your mind. He taught us all the different subjects. Math, history, biology, languages, physical education and no matter what he taught us, he managed to put some magic in what he taught and that made it special. That is what great teachers are able to do. It was then that I decided that I too wanted to be a teacher. It seems to me that the most rewarding thing that I can do in life is to teach children. If I can have the same dedication and level of enthusiasm and skill that Mr. Rommel has then I will feel completely fulfilled. Mom and Dad have different ideas.

"No son of mine will be a teacher. It is below your intellectual capacity. You are too smart to be a teacher. A doctor is what you must be," says Dad. Flattered that they feel I have the capacity to be a doctor, at first, I embrace the idea. Then after a while realizing that I do not really want to be a doctor, I tell them so.

Dad's reply: "Do you think that I am spending thousands of francs a year, to provide you with a private education, so that you can waste it on becoming a teacher. You must be daft. It is beneath you. We want you to be a doctor and that's final." This is the thing I hate the most about him. What he says goes. There is no room for negotiation. My opinion counts for nothing. It is so unfair and it insults my sensibilities. With them, what matters is how we look to the outside world. It's never about me and always about them. If my real Mom and Dad were here they would listen to me and support me, I'm sure. That's what real parents do, they encourage their children. I am resentful of their controlling ways; always telling what I can cannot do. I wish they'd get killed in a car crash or something. That would serve them right.

CHAPTER 44

Good news arrives from Canada. Maurice wrote me that he will come to Belgium for vacation. It's been five years since he left and I can't wait to see him again. On the day of his arrival we drive to Melsbroek, near Brussels, to pick him up. It takes me some time to recognize him when we meet up in the arrival hall. He is a man now; wearing a brightly coloured shirt and a cap he looks every bit like an American, not a Canadian. We hug. He has a lot of luggage. "Presents for everyone" he says.

"Speak English, Maurice," I ask. He does, but what comes out does not sound like Gary Cooper in "Friendly Persuasion" or Humphrey Bogart in "Casablanca". Maurice talks English and then ends most sentences with an "eh". That's what Canadian sounds like I suppose. Anyway it's pretty cool that my big brother speaks English. Maurice has never been much good at letter writing, so we've got a lot of catching up to do about his experiences in Canada. He tells us that when he first arrived in Canada, he was staying with Auntie Saar and Uncle Jonas. They live in Toronto and they have a flower store aptly named "The Dutch Flower Shoppe". After all they are Dutch, you know. After a mutual disagreement, as he puts it, he decides that he wants to live with Uncle Levie and Auntie Roo and Loukie. His clothes are oddly different from what we wear here. His suit jacket has only one button and the pants are wide around the knee and tapers down severely at the ankle. The whole suit fits quite loose and sort of hangs on the body.

Maurice says "They call it the Zoot suit and its cool man. We can watch TV from early morning to late night." Here TV starts broadcasting at 8pm and stops at 11pm. What can they possibly show all day every day? They must run out of news.

Maurice settles in the dull routine of every day life. He decides to extend his vacation, much to my delight. He was only going to stay for a few weeks and since he does not have a job to return to, he now wants to remain in Belgium for an indefinite period.

"Dad asks "Do you want to help me in my flower business for a while? I'll pay you a wage. Maurice accepts the offer. He drives the truck and really does not mind getting up at the beastly hour of 4am. Friday nights, freshly groomed and smelling of Old Spice, he goes out to Antwerp, "for fun and fuck" he quips. "Man cannot live on fun alone.

"Can I drive the Oldsmobile Dad? He asks

"No, son you can take the truck."

"That's not hip." So he takes the train instead.

"Make sure you catch the last train. It leaves the station at midnight, Dad yells after him.

With a nonchalant wave over his shoulder Maurice serves notice that he has no intention of being back on the last train. He's been in Canada too long and enjoyed unfettered liberty to let a train stop him from having fun, he tells me.

He misses the last train and sleeps on a bench in the railway station, waiting for the first train to Kapellen at 5am. He does not mention the fact that he sleeps over at a girl's house waiting for the train. It's always the same. He runs out of excuses. Dad is pissed. Nobody ever dares to disobey him. Maurice doesn't seem to mind the ranting of the lunatic.

"What girl, what's her name," I ask.

"It's not the same girl every time. There's plenty of choice, Jackie." Oh, how I envy him.

"In Canada I can do what I want, nobody cares what time I get home. I've been going it since I was fifteen. No big deal." He is twenty years old and figures that he is old enough to make his own decisions.

Dad offers this ultimatum: "You live under my roof and you do as I say. Otherwise you can go on your way."

"I can't live under a dictatorship. I don't know how much more I can take of this," Maurice declares one day.

I learn to speak some English. Not enough to carry on a conversation though.

My departure day for Colomendy has arrived. None to soon, I dare say. Things are getting pretty tenuous at home. All the kids gather at the Lycée at 7am this Saturday morning. We board a charter bus for the trip to Oostende. There are 19 of us, ten boys and nine girls. From Oostende we board the ferry that will take us across the English Channel to Dover. The ship is much larger than I imagined. It can accommodate 200 cars and about 700 passengers. The captain goes through a drill, explaining how to put on a life jacket in the case of an emergency.

"It's just routine folks," he explains, "No need to worry. Haven't lost any passengers in a fortnight."

What's a fortnight? I hope that there are enough life jackets. The trip across the channel takes about two hours. The sea is pretty rough and some of us are seasick. I am not, but don't ask me to eat a bacon sandwich, my stomach feels queasy. I'd woof my cookies if I ate anything. The trip ends not a moment too soon. I feel the motion of the boat for the next while, even on solid ground. We lug our suitcases to the train station across the street and board the train to London, where we will be staying for a few days. From there we'll travel to Liverpool. After a two hour train ride we arrive in London's Victoria station. It's one of the hottest days on record. A muggy 30 degrees makes me shvitz as never before. We don't have days like these in Belgium. Our chaperons, with all of us in tow, are in search of a bar where we can have a cold beer. We find one inside the station. What a welcome sight.

"A round of Guinness please," says Mr. Dumphrey, our male chaperon, in impeccable British English. The waiter returns with our beers. I take a big swig right away. It's horrible; the beer is served at room temperature, and so on a 30-degree day it's like drinking warm water. What's the matter with the British? Never heard of ice-cold beer? Despite the fact that the beer is warm, it does quench my thirst and it gives me a buzz.

We have to lug our baggage again as we head for the nearest taxi stand. The taxis are strange contraptions. They look like square boxes, model A Ford look, and the driver is separated from the passengers. The steering wheel is on the right hand side of the car and all traffic drives along the left side of the street, opposite to the way it is in Belgium and Holland. The British like to do things different. We hire five taxis and the chaperons give the drivers an address in Hyde Park, It's a short cab ride from the station and after only a few minutes we arrive at a large imposing building that is operated as a youth hostel. The boys are put up on the 2nd floor and the girls have rooms on the 3rd floor. We are cautioned that we have to stay on our own floors. There is a common room on the first floor where everybody can gather to chat, play cards and other games. We are all pretty tired from the traveling all day and we retire. In the middle of the night some of us boys decide to climb the fire escape up to the third floor. We surprise the girls as we climb into their room through the open window. We stay around for quite a while. Some of the boys and girls are fooling around, groping and kissing in the dark. I can hear the muffled giggles. Suddenly the door opens and the hostel manager stands in the doorway, yelling at us to get out. We escape out the open window figuring that we are safe and nothing more but a caution will come of this. Little do we know that when the guy said to get out he meant that he wanted us all out of the hostel that very moment. Its 3am, where are we're going to go at this time of night in a strange city. The chaperons are awakened and told the gory details of our escapade. They plead with the manager for one more chance. He relents and allows us to stay for the rest of the night, but we must leave in the morning, he says. Much sobered by the experience we don't feel so adventurous now and slink back to our room. In the morning instead of going sight seeing we spend our time looking for other accommodations. We manage to find a small hotel that agrees to put us up for the next few nights. It is still in the Hyde Park district, close to Soho, a not so safe area.

"Don't go out by yourselves. Go in pairs, if you must. Don't go wandering. Better yet. Stay in the hotel. It's much safer," the chaperons caution. We manage to sneak out and wind up in one of the local bars. Only about seven of us were brave enough to venture out tonight. We order drinks and it seems pleasant enough. Fats Domino's Blueberry Hill is playing on the jukebox and we are enjoying watching these guys play billiards. We talk amongst ourselves, Smalltalk mostly. Someone tells a joke and we all laugh. Boy, that's a mistake. One of the billiards playing guys stops playing and walks over to our table. He grabs a hold of my collar and asks me something I can't understand. I nearly shit in my pants. He asks me again and with added emphasis he turns my collar so that I can barely breathe.

"Are you picking on me?" he screams. Francisco, who speaks English, answers him back and the fellow lets go of my collar, dusts me off and asks if he can buy us a drink.

"What did you say to him?" I ask quietly.

"I told him you were an idiot and that you were deaf and dumb, so now he feels really bad and wants to make amends."

"Gee thanks." Now these guys are our best friends all of a sudden and they won't let us leave until the place closes at 4am. At the end of the night I realize that people from Soho are pretty nice. The beers helped make up my mind. I can barely walk back to the hotel. It was a fun night, though it started out pretty crappy. The hotel door is locked and we have to ring the bell for the night clerk to let us in. Thank goodness the chaperones are nowhere to be seen. It appears that they did not see us sneak out. It's already light out. The sun is just coming up. Hung over and with a pounding headache we go see the sights. We go to Piccadilly Circus, Trafalgar Square, Buckingham Palace and the Tower of London. The chaperones question us about where we went last night. They said that had done a bed check and found us gone. They did not appear too concerned and we told them our adventure. Of course Francisco had to tell them that I nearly got killed and how he managed to save my life. After three fun-filled days we leave London. It is a long 4-hour train ride to Liverpool. We pass the time by telling tall stories and jokes and playing cards. In Liverpool a bus awaits to take us to Colomendy.

I like one of the girls from the college, we sit together and I put my arm over her shoulder. She does not seem to mind, my hand lingers over her breast and at first my hand brushes her breast in a careless way. She leaves it there and when I work up enough courage to grab her breast I can feel her shudder. I leave my hand there for the rest of the ride because I don't know what else to do. I get a cramp in my arm but I dare not move it.

The entrance to the camp, off the main street is somewhat hidden. A small sign warns the traveler to be on the lookout for Camp Colomendy. An arched gate allows the bus traffic to enter. We travel along a narrow trail for what seems forever. The road is well traveled and full of rain filled bone-jarring potholes. Tall conifers line the roadway; further in the underbrush is thick and impenetrable. Here and there we can discern walking trails cut out of the thick brush. The weather is overcast and the sky is gray. Even though it is the middle of summer we have to wear sweaters to keep warm. When we get to the camp I have a terrible pain in my lower stomach, I can barely walk. It is that painful. The pain goes right into my testicles. I have never experienced anything quite like it.

When I tell Francisco he says;"You got lover's nuts because you did not come, you'll have to jerk off when you get to the sleeping barracks." I don't think I can wait that long, the pain is unbearable. We are assigned sleeping quarters in one of the cabins. It is a large cabin that sleeps 15 of us. We take our suitcases from the bus to the cabin. It takes all my effort because walking in my condition is so difficult. I run to the bathroom to take care of the business at hand. The girls are assigned a different cabin. The showers and WC's are in the next building, I rush to get my business taken care of. Feeling somewhat relieved it still hurts like the dickens. If we have to go to the toilet in the middle of the night we have to go outside and cross over to the next building.

Kids, in the camp come from all parts of Europe, Spain, Portugal, France, Italy, Germany, Belgium, Holland, Sweden, Denmark, Norway, Finland, the British Isles and Switzerland. We register with the camp director and his staff. Our names are ticked off the master list and we receive a weekly schedule that outlines the events for the two weeks that we will be there. On the back of the schedule is a map of the camp. How useful is this? It shows where the girls' cabins are located. Every day, in the dining/entertainment hall, we get a camp newsletter with a daily update and newsworthy gossip. Who writes this stuff? It's all about how you define fun, I suppose. At first we're shy to mingle with kids from other countries, so we stay in our own groups. The camp director, Mr. H.H. Blissett runs the summer camp. "Call me Mr. Blissett," he says, Mr. Blissett, his voice somewhat high pitched, launches into his official welcome speech.

"Welcome boys and girls. We have come together in this camp called Colomendy to partake in two weeks of camaraderie and fun activities. Little is known of Colomendy before 1700. Not even where the dovecote stood, which gave Colomendy its name. Richard Wilson, Wales' first and greatest landscape painter, visited Colomendy many times in the eighteenth century where his cousin, Catherine Jones lived. Wilson himself lived at Colomendy in 1782, the year he died. Wilson's painting of the Pen y Garreg Wen and Loggerheads', now in the Tate Gallery, was almost certainly sketched during his time at Colomendy."

"What the heck is he talking about?" It sounds like a guttural mumbo-jumbo. Even Francisco, who speaks fluent English, has trouble translating. "I don't know what he's saying guys."

Mr. Blissett continues, undaunted," The Colomendy experience is unique and is an important aspect of your education. The camp has approximately 30 cabins and each cabin accommodates 15 kids. Please wear your name badges so that others will know who we are and what country you are from. I will assign one of my staff members to each cabin. It's not that we don't trust you. But we don't want wild parties in the dormitories, do we? It's lights out at 10pm. Breakfast will be served starting at 7am and will continue until 9am. Lunch will be served starting at 12noon and will continue until 1pm. Supper will be starting at 5 pm till 6pm. Each cabin is assigned to the duty roster for cleaning the dining hall and serving the meals. The dining hall must be completely cleaned by 8pm to accommodate the night festivities."

Will announces that tonight is a dance night. It's a night for everyone to get acquainted. The following night is when we start a talent show. Each of us is asked to perform something. It could be a skit or story telling. Or we could sing. Anyways everybody has to perform something nobody is exempted. We are to do it in groups and the cabins will be competing for points against one another. So whatever we do we do it for the honour of the cabin. Beside the Belgian contingent we also have one Spanish boy and five boys from Holland. Since the Dutch speak a similar language as the Belgians, albeit with a different accent, we have no trouble understanding each other. The Spanish boy is named Joaquin and he is from Barcelona. He is a few years older than most of us and since they both speak Spanish he gets along with Francisco. We have a cabin conference to try to figure out what we will be performing for talent night. The Dutch have already decided that they will perform a skit by themselves and they don't require our help. Joaquin is an accomplished classical guitarist and has already entertained us with his brilliant virtuosity. He decides that he will play a classical piece on talent night. We settle on playing and lip-syncing along with Bill Hailey and his Comets. We will be singing and playing to the song. "See you later Alligator" I'll be playing the "air guitar". The night of the dance brings many surprises. Firstly, because of Francisco's dare-do he and I meet two beautiful Swedish girls named Bibi and Irene. Both hail from Stockholm and they speak passable English. It does not matter to me since I don't understand English too well. So we speak a combination of German, French and English. Francisco likes Bibi, she resembles Elke Sommers. I really like Irene; her face is somewhat rounder with a very pretty nose and blue eyes. I can't help but notice her perky breasts through her tight fitting sweater. We hit it off really well and since they are playing slow dances we stay on the dance floor and dance very close. I get excited and she notices it and pushes harder into me. Never have I felt so daring and before I know it we are kissing each other on the mouth. She opens her lips and I play with her tongue. This is the first time I have ever French kissed. Her tongue and mouth are so soft. I can't believe my good fortune. Will comes over and taps me on the shoulder and whispers: "Hey cool it buddy." The last dance of the night is a slow song by The Diamonds "Why Do Fools Fall in Love" a very appropriate title because by the end of the evening I am madly smitten with Irene. I go to bed with sore balls.

The next morning I can't wait to meet up with Irene. I throw on some clothes and walk over the WC. Building for my ablutions and teeth brushing. There is a lineup to use the toilets and everyone in line curses the guys in front of him in the toilets for being way to slow. The showers work but there is no hot water left. I guess tomorrow I'll have to get up a lot earlier if I want to have a hot shower. With the essential washing and brushing duties out of the way, we all head over to the dining hall and anticipate that the day will be filled with fun. It starts out rather strange. None of us are used to English menus. We have a choice of porridge, which none of us being from Belgium, have ever heard of, or cold serials with strange names. Kellogg's Corn Flakes and Rice Crispies. None of it rings a bell with any of us. We have to content ourselves with cold toast and eggs, scrambled please and pancakes with syrup! Irene enters the hall and my heart skips a beat. She comes over to the table where we are sitting and she gives me a peck on the cheek. She gets herself some toast and coffee and she sits down at our table. Her friend Bibi has also arrived and she sits with us, close to Francisco. They are so in love. With breakfast done it is our turn to clean up. The ten of us from Belgium are charged with the duty of cleaning up the mess hall. Removing the dishes, cleaning the tables and the floor and then doing the dishes prove to be quite a chore. By ten am, we are finished. Bibi and Irene, tired of waiting for us have gone off with their friends to sight see around the immediate countryside. Somewhat disappointed we decide to stay around the camp and rehearse the skit that we will be performing tonight. After playing the record a few times and us playing along on our imaginary instruments we are now fully confident that tonight we'll walk away with first prize. To our dismay we find that on the night of the performances no less than three other groups are doing exactly the same thing that we are. The others seem to put much more passion and artistry in their performances than we do and we have to content ourselves with fourth prize. Some kids are very talented and funny as they do skits and jokes. It is a fun-filled night and people are really getting to know and enjoy each other. Irene and I and Francisco and Bibi go out into the dark night to smooch.

The following day a group of us decide that we will climb the Snowdon, a local mountain, in the area. It is the first sunny day we experience since arriving in England. A bus from the camp takes us to the foot of the mountain and we set off on our climb, the ascension of Snowdon Mountain, North Wales highest elevation. It takes us about fifteen minutes of arduous climbing to reach the top. When we reach the peak we spend ten minutes basking in our glory, feeling like Edmund Hillary when he reached the summit of Mount Everest. We have a bagged lunch that we devour in no time. Climbing is such hard work. Then it's back to camp and new adventures to experience and places to conquer. Irene wants to go to the village next to the camp. The village is called Mold. We have to walk out from the camp to the main road where we can then catch the local bus that takes us to the village. It is starting to rain again, a steady drizzle that soaks one to the bone. Irene brought her umbrella and we both stay dry by huddling under it. I kind of like the feeling of being so close with her. She smells good. Francisco and Bibi have come along. The bus ride lasts about ten minutes. Mold boasts a five and ten cent store called Woolworth's. In Belgium we don't have these types of stores. Probably because everything costs more than five or ten cents. We go into the store; more to keep warm and it gives us something to do on this dreary day. We stand in a portal kissing. Working up enough courage to rub her breast through her raincoat is definitely the highlight of my day. I don't know what the next step is from hereon in.

Francisco tells me "take her to bed, man." That's easy for him to say, he's done it many times before, but I would not know where to start. For the time being I am content to remain in the groping stage of our relationship. Going to bed will have to wait. It is time to return to camp. All in all it's been a good day. Back at camp we have supper. Boiled meat and cabbage is hardly the fare I'm used to. One thing is for sure, English cooking is different. Being used to eating fine French cuisine, these meals are quite a change. Day in and day out the meals don't improve, same fare, an insult to a palate that was raised on French gastronomique. We make do with toast and eggs. At night I eat only desserts, rice pudding or different kinds of pies.

Days and nights are loaded with activities. We don't have a moment to ourselves. Will and his staff do a masterful job at keeping us busy. My romance with Irene has blossomed to heavy petting underneath the clothing and we both are quite satisfied with that. Neither of us has a burning desire to go beyond that point.

The end of our stay comes far too soon. Irene and I pledge our eternal love for each other. We exchange addresses and promise to write every day. We travel together on the train trip form Liverpool to London, an unexpected bonus for both of us. As we part company at Victoria Station we promise again to write every day. It hurts to leave her because this is the first time in my life that I have experienced such intense love and I want to hold on to it. The rest of my voyage back is rather melancholy. Being without Irene is rather overwhelming. I am not sure I can cope with this. From the recesses of my mind shades of a similar sense of loss resurface. I've trained myself to remain unaffected, but here it is, I can let it destroy me or will myself to not feel anything. I chose the latter.

The trip across the channel is not quite as eventful as it was on the way down. The sea in the channel is calm and nobody gets seasick. Back in Oostende, Maurice is waiting for me. There is no one else with him because the rest of the family is still on vacation in France.

"Jackie, how was your trip? Did you enjoy yourself? What did you do every day?" The questions keep coming. Like a bad record that's stuck in the same spot and plays the same piece of music over and over. I don't feel like sharing any of it with him at this moment. Maybe after a while, when the hurt wears off and I don't feel so sad, I'll be able to share. The long drive back is spent in almost total silence. Maurice feels my reluctance to speak and he respects my privacy. The events of the past month have

Dad has left Maurice in charge of the business and even though he calls Maurice on a daily basis, for updates the business proceeds well in Maurice's capable hands. With a few weeks left of my summer vacation I am able to help him with the business. We drive to Holland twice a week and visit the customers twice a week. Its hard work but we have much fun together. We enjoy each other's company. For the first time I feel like I really have a brother who'll stay with me for a long time. Since Mom, Dad and Juliana are away we go to Antwerp several times. What freedom. So on Saturday nights we go dancing. The girls really like Maurice, especially when he speaks English. The only drawback is that we have to travel in the truck. You can't really show off in a truck that has "Bloemen van Nebig" (Nebig Flowers) written on the side of it. While Mom and Dad are away we need not worry about curfews. Life is peaceful. Nobody to yell at us or tell us what to do or when to do. It's great. Why can't it be like this all the time? We spend every waking moment in each other's company. We always speak English so my language skills are vastly improved. I train every day to speak the way Americans speak. The girls love it.

CHAPTER 45

Erik and Maurice have made plans to travel to Sweden together. They will be camping for two weeks and the mode of travel is Erik's Vespa scooter, the ultimate consumer cool. So the two set off on one misty summer morning, packed to overflowing on their great adventure. I lobbied to go along, but I probably had a better chance to travel to the moon on camelback.

Dad says, "No and that's final."

My final argument is a deal breaker,"I've been to Colomendy on my own and everything turned out fine!" Now he's really upset. I can kick myself. I shouldn't have reminded him. He refuses to even entertain the idea. I figure that at age seventeen I should have a certain level of independence and be away from parental scrutiny if even for one moment.

As the long summer of 1957 ends and memories start to fade into fall, I realize now that most experiences in my short but eventful life are not memories but that they are experiences staged in time that needed immediate attention, and therefore were not allowed to linger into memories. In contemplation of this I feel that something in my life is missing. No warm fuzzy feelings to think back upon. No cozy moments by a fire, no loving embraces from parents or gentle scolding for having done something wrong. The ingredients that make up life's memories are missing. And worst of all there is no one to share anything with and that makes me sad. Yet, I should feel happy. I live in a nice stable environment. My life, though restricted, is not bad. Everything required is provided for. I want for nothing, except that one ingredient that gets me misty eyed whenever I think about it. The irreplaceable smothering embrace from my Mother.

Laughter can lessen a burden, or put things that are otherwise too horrible to contemplate in a different light. The best medicine is to be able to laugh at one-self, not in a way to poke fun at someone's shortcomings but rather laughing at yourself because of your own shortcomings. Jewish humor is just that. Come to think of it, Jewish humour is only funny if told by another Jew. In other words gentiles should refrain from telling Jewish jokes. That is not funny and is often felt as being anti-Semitic. Some non-Jewish, so-called friends, knowing that I am Jewish, will tell me Jewish jokes and laugh themselves at the punch line. They stare at me because I don't laugh.

"Don't you get it?" they query.

"Yes I do, but the way you tell it, it's not funny."

"I tell it exactly like Max Tailleur told it."

"When Max Tailleur, the Jewish comedian, with special emphasis on the Jewish tells, then it's funny. When you tell it it's an insult to Jews." I explain.

Self conscious about their faux pas, the lame excuse is always the same, "Boy, you Jews are too sensitive. Some of my best friends are Jewish." I cannot even get angry at the insensitivity anymore. The subtlety of the humour is wasted on them. All they understand is the grossness of the punch line.

My favourite humourist of all times is Meyer Sluyser. He is a Dutch broadcast journalist and he wrote about Jewish life in Amsterdam. "Mr. Monday and Other Tales of Jewish Amsterdam" written by him is a tale worth reading. Besides Sluyser, who really is not a comedian but a Jewish chronicler that happens to be very funny, there are Jewish comedians that are worthy of mention, Max Tailleur, an Amsterdam born Jew, is one of them. He has his own club in the center of Amsterdam and he always plays to full houses. On the rare occasions that he performs elsewhere tickets are forever at a premium. He plays to a wider audience, besides Jewish people, his comedy is universally understood and most times tells about the pathos of Jewish life. Some Jewish critics claim that he exploits the Jewish plight for profit, but I don't think so. Jewish history, particularly Amsterdam Jewish history, intertwined with life in the "Jordaan", the name given to a region in Amsterdam downtown, is unique replete with its own characters and stories. Johnny Jordaan and Tante Leen are two performers that kind of immortalized life in the Jordaan, in song and dance.

Eric and Maurice returned from their trip after two weeks, excited and full of marvelous stories of Casanova-like proportions. I don't know how much is fact and how much of it is fiction. Based on who is telling the stories, though, I must believe that most of it is true because Eric is the storyteller. He is in absolute awe of Maurice's prowess with the girls. "Maurice is amazing" he marvels. They traveled a total of 3,000 km. on the Vespa scooter. Not the most comfortable mode of travel,"but the memories are unforgettable" they both admit. The first day of their departure they went all the way to Hamburg in Germany and camped at a local campground. The following day they left early and traveled to Puttgarden and waited for the ferry to take them across into Denmark the next morning. They then traveled to Helsingborg-Helsingor and another ferry took them across to Sweden and from there to Stockholm. Eric said everywhere they went the girls were friendly and had no qualms about staying in the same tent with Maurice and him. Every night they hooked up with different girls. Gosh, how I wish I could have been there.

CHAPTER 46

The school year starts out with the pleasant anticipation of shiny newness. "Happy to see you man", is my new greeting to Francisco and my other friends. Eager to show off my new language skills I converse only in English now. We compare notes on how the rest of our summers were spent. He went back to Columbia for a visit and brought me back a multi coloured poncho. Merton Dodge and his family spent time back in Paterson, New Jersey. He tells me about all the news in the United States. Ford introduces a new car called the Edsel. It is quite a novelty and very revolutionary for its time. The hula-hoop is the favourite toy for girls and Ricky Nelson is the new American heartthrob. Dwight D. Eisenhower, the supreme commander of the Allied forces and chief liberator of Europe, is the President of the United States. Merton mentions the Civil Rights movement and the Montgomery bus boycott in Little Rock, Arkansas. The Civil Rights and busing issues seem important to him but to me, living in Belgium does not seem that important. He says; "Now you can maybe understand why Americans were not that emotionally affected by what happened to the Jews in Europe. We could not fully identify with the gravity of the situation." I never quite looked at it that way, figuring that everyone in the entire world would have felt our hurt.

Juan Emmanuel Fangio, the Argentinean born racecar driver, wins the German Grand prix race again and is considered by many as the best racecar driver the sport has ever seen. Jacques Anquetil wins the Tour De France bicycle race. Real Madrid wins the European soccer championship yet again.

I am still sending letters to Irene regularly professing my undying love for her. The response from her is somewhat tardy and lukewarm. Memories fade and in the end we stop corresponding altogether. Both of us come to the realization that long distance romances rarely work. School takes up most of my time. The home work load is staggering. Even for me, that tries to get by on the bare minimum of work, it still takes several hours per night to complete. I don't like school particularly, it bores me. I still manage to get scores in the high 80's but I know that I can do much better if I only applied myself. Spending most of my time at school, not to do work but spending time with my friends, allows me to avoid the glare of scrutiny from Mom and Dad. They are far too occupied, anyways, to spend much time worrying about what I do.

Luc is away at boarding school. I miss him. His father insists that he must become an officer in the Belgian merchant fleet so he goes to a private naval academy for officer training. Dad is mad at the Kiekens family for having slighted him and he now proclaims he'll have nothing to do with them ever again.

"I don't want you to talk with Luc or his family ever again." he threatens me.

"But Luc is my best friend."

"I don't care!" he screams. He scares me so in order not to cause him any more aggravation I decide to let things cool off for the next little while. Luc is gone for the following few months, regardless. Dad also has a falling out with the van Emden's. He threatens us all, on the pain of death, not to associate with those people anymore. His expectation of people is too high, I feel, and impossible for anyone to live up to. When he is offended by someone he never forgives them. It's hard on us all.

The Brussels world's fair, Expo 58, will be starting on April 17, 1958. It has been years in the planning and it will showcase Belgium and in particular Brussels to the rest of the world. Nearly 15,000 workers spent three years building the 2 km² site, found on the Heysel plateau, seven kilometres northwest of Brussels . The site stands out for a giant sculpture of an atom, called the Atomium.

There is a restaurant in the top sphere of the Atomium. Many countries have their own pavilions and the building trades are busy. Trying to get someone to come and fix anything at this time is impossible. You have to wait months to get anyone to come. It is the first major world expo after World War II, the previous world's fair having been the 1939 New York World's Fair. More than 42 million visitors will visit the site, which is opened with a call for world peace and social and economic progress, issued by King Baudouin.

It was an exciting year for movies, though they were not masterpieces, they were entertaining. Nevertheless, Gigi with Leslie Caron and Maurice Chevalier is amongst one of my favourites. The new movie star sensation, Elvis Presley, has made another movie, King Creole, which I really like. It tells the story of a young, tough musician making his way in New Orleans, and is an adaptation of Harold Robbins' novel "A stone for Danny Fisher".

Maurice takes me to visit the Expo and I taste my very first milk shake at the American pavilion. For the first time I hear Stereo Hi-Fi music which sounds like hearing the music live in a concert hall. We spent the whole day walking around the Expo site. In the end we've only seen a small part of Expo. We are both suitably overwhelmed with the new design, innovations and inventions that promise to make the future much more exciting than it already is. The Russians are featuring Sputnik I, the first rocket that went up into space. The Soviet Union made history on October 4, 1957, when they successfully launched Sputnik I. The world's first satellite is about the size of a basketball, weighing only 183 pounds, and it takes only about 98 minutes to orbit the Earth on an elliptical path. That launch brings in a new political, military, technological, and scientific race between Russia and the United States. The Americans have tried several times, each time unsuccessfully, to launch a rocket into orbit around the earth. The American pavilion features many new time-saving inventions and I have my first attempt at twirling a hula-hoop around my waist. The American girls demonstrate how easy it is, however most people, including me, are singularly unsuccessful at doing it for more than ten seconds.

CHAPTER 47

Maurice has decided that he cannot stay in Belgium any longer. Even the promise of inheriting the profitable flower business cannot induce him to change his mind. Dad is just too tyrannical for his now independent mind. He is trying to convince me to go back to Canada with him. "In Canada we'll be on our own. We'll be able to do what we want, with no one to tell we can't do this or that." he explains. It sure sounds inviting. "I want to be brutally frank with you and I hope you will not get too upset when I tell you this. Our mom and Dad will not be coming back, so therefore it makes no sense to hang around Belgium anymore. You might me as well stop hoping and get used to the idea." My first reaction is anger. "How do you know that?" I scream, with tears in my eyes. "Nobody knows for sure that they died in the concentration camp, you said so yourself many times."

"We've got to go on with our lives and start to live for ourselves now and we can't do that if we stay in Belgium with these people. They will kill our spirit." The sense of impending adventure intrigues me, so I tell him that I will think about it and give him my answer in the next few days.

"I'm going back to Canada, with or without you." he threatens. The next few days are hell. My feelings are ambivalent. They have been good to me and treated me like a son. They have given me everything that money can buy. Provided me with the best education and given me tools with which to make something of myself in this world. What has been lacking in my upbringing is the sense of individuality. I bear no deep seated grudges and nothing urges me to share any deep feelings with them, least of all the feelings that I have kept hidden, even from myself, for so long. My sense of loss for my own parents is so painful and there is no respite. Life goes on as if nothing has happened of note. Bottled up emotion has shaped my attitude towards them and the rest of the world. It is easier to keep things inside than to share it. The feelings of isolation are worsening without my ability to grasp the reason for it. No one is there to make any sense of it and it is allowed to fester deep within me. We never talk about the war, my parents, the war's consequences and the biggest question of all. Why was it allowed to happen? There is nobody to answer any questions and all the while I feel that many things that happened were probably my fault.

I tell Maurice that I will be going back to Canada with him. He says: "Great, you've made the right decision; we'll have so much fun together in Canada. You will really like the life there. Now comes the biggest hurdle of all and that is to tell Mom and Dad and Juliana the news. All day I have been waiting for the right moment to tell them. At the dinner table, with trepidation, I broach the subject.

"Mom and Dad, Maurice, as you know, is going back to Canada and he asked me to go with him and I have accepted." I blurt out. Well the reaction my announcement was nothing short of the advent of world war III. Dad starts to yell at me: "You ingrate, after all we have done for you, that is how you repay us?" He roars. His harangue goes on for another half hour and I am getting rather scared that he is going to attack me, just as he did Raymond when he attempted to leave. He does not pick up a knife. In the end he screams:" Now I want you out of the house as quickly as possible, you are not our son, you never were, and even if you change your mind you are not welcome in this house any longer. If you change your mind we will put you in an orphanage." Mom and Juliana are crying and they say nothing. Of course I am upset at this turn of events. I had hoped for some level of understanding. Some disappointment maybe and some complaining about my ingratitude, but never that I am no longer wanted. "What will you use for money to pay for your fare?" he demands. The question did not occur to me until he asked it. Not knowing what to say it is probably better to remain quiet at this juncture. All the while Maurice just sits there and dad just glares at him. "It's your entire fault. You fill your brother with all those stupid ideas. Look what you've done. You two get out of my site. I don't want to see you two anymore." And with that he storms out of the dining room leaving his plate of food untouched. None of us are hungry. I don't know what to say, so I stay at the table, forced to listen to the sobbing noises. We get up from the table, clear the dishes still full of food and everyone retires into their own thoughts for the night. Pondering the reaction of my revelation I wonder at the wisdom of my decision. Feeling rather guilty I try to avoid Juliana's accusatory looks. Surely she feels betrayed, her eyes encountering mine are asking; "why?" She knows the answer to that question. Life with Dad has never been a picnic. His authoritarian ways are vexatious to the spirit and his lack of trust in us is the very reasons that cause me to bolt from here and escape to freedom. Typically from Mom's viewpoint, she feels betrayed and as much as I would like to reassure her that my decision was not based on her treatment of me, it is rather a mute point. "What's the difference?" I ask myself. "We're leaving anyways. The die has been cast and it can't be undone. We've got to go on from here. The rest of the night is spent in quiet, although it is only nine o'clock we all go to our own beds. Sleep does not come easily. I toss and turn and think of what I've done and what we'll have to endure for the rest of our stay here. It won't be easy. Dad is pretty vindictive. For the following few weeks Maurice and I engage a myriad of activities. No one in the house really talks to us anymore and it is decided that in order for me to finance my trip to Canada I am now indentured to the Nebig family until I leave some six months from now. Meanwhile I paint the laundry room, kitchen, several bedrooms and even the brick on the outside of the house receives my artistic touch with whitewash. Painting is not on my list of favourite things to do. It's tedious and I'm pretty lousy at it.

We travel to the Canadian embassy for the long awaited interview with a Canadian immigration officer. Thank goodness he speaks French, so I have no difficulty communicating with him. He asks the customary questions, I suppose they are customary. When we get to the spot where he asks why I am going to Canada and what I will be doing there my answer is "Student, I am going to school in Canada" I proclaim. He shoots me a horrified look and tells me that I'll never get in to Canada as a student.

"We don't need students in Canada; we've got plenty of those right now, of our own. We need workers; it's a young country and a very large country. What are you good at?" Maurice and I look at each other and almost simultaneously we say "Painting."

"Very good, we need painters in Canada. Now do you have a job waiting for you in Canada?"

Maurice nods: "With Harry Turfryer. That is where I work as a house painter." While the officer is busy writing down the answers I shoot Maurice a quizzical look and he nods enthusiastically.

"Who the hell is Harry Turfryer?" I ask myself. After about one hour the interview is over and the officer says that we now have to wait for another six months while they process the paper work.

"Six months?" I panic.

"Yes, that is if nothing goes wrong," is his stoic reply. On the way out of the embassy, Maurice explains that in Canada he is a house painter and his boss is really, Harry Turfryer. And here I thought he was lying through his teeth.

"Can you imagine the hell we'll have to live through for the next months?" I wonder out loud.

"Don't worry" is Maurice's favourite answer. Somehow I can't help but be very worried. I know Dad and his anger.

At home they keep on dreaming up more chores for us to do. Thank goodness dad is away most of the time. I don't know where he goes but frankly, I don't much care, so long as I don't have to face him. Mom on her own is almost civil to me, while Juliana keeps telling me how unfair it is that she has to stay with them on her own without my support. I really feel pretty bad about that. I realize now that, after working like a slave for the past few months that I had a pretty cushy life before. There were no great expectations for jobs to do around the house; we had servants that looked after the household chores and the gardens. Now I am mowing the lawns, raking leaves, taking out the garbage and, oh ya, endless painting. There is an end to this somewhere, because I can't see me spending the rest of my days working like a dog and being treated worse than one. One day, the long awaited manila envelope arrives bearing the Canadian embassy insignia on it. We cannot wait to open it. We are told we cannot open until dad is home. He will open it and tell us what's in it. Dad puts in an appearance that particular night and with a grave look on his face, opens the envelope. He stares at it for what seems an eternity. Nobody talks. Nervously I listen to the Westminster chime clock tick off the minutes. He says nothing. He just sits there and stares. When the clock strikes eight I nearly jump out of my skin. He takes off his reading glasses and looks me straight in the eye and finally says very calmly "Well, you're going to Canada, I guess." My feelings are ambivalent at this point. I wish I could stay in Belgium and yet I want to go to Canada. What I would like the most is for him to say: "I forgive you my son and good luck on your great journey" All he does is stare at me, wistfully, without uttering a further word. Mom says sardonically: "You got what you wanted; I hope you know what you've done. You've ripped this family apart and now you're walking away from the consequences. I hope you're happy." Tears well up in my eyes and though I want her to comfort me and tell me everything is going to be OK she walks away at a time when I need her most. Life is cruel like that, I suppose. Deep in the recesses of my mind, I feel like I've been in this same place before. The feeling is eerily familiar and most of all; I can't help but think that what is happening here is inevitable. That good things are temporal and must end, because that's the way my life is. Don't ever get accustomed to things remaining as they are. Maurice, being more pragmatic than me, feels good about the outcome. He figures he got what he wanted, damn the consequences, let's get on with life. I wish I could be so detached. I worry too much me suppose, but that's the way I am, steeped in guilt and I don't know why. The airline tickets have been purchased and the date of departure is May 18, 1958. As the prophetic day arrives I am not feeling very proud for what I have wrought and each one, Mom, Dad and Juliana ensure that I am reminded of this fact at every instant of my waking moments.

"Parting is such sweet sorrow" is a line from a Shakespeare play, I believe. No sweet sorrow fills my heart. Instead my heart feels just like a lump of coal, dark, heavy and cold. Why do I feel so darn guilty? This is what I've wanted, isn't it?

The dreaded morning has arrived and we bid each other a tearful goodbye. Juliana embraces me.

"I love you Jackie." she whispers. "I'll never forget you. Please write every day." Mom and dad each stand off to the side and watch the goings on. When I approach them to attempt to say something, they both turn on their heels and leave the room without uttering a sound. Figuring that I am dismissed, Maurice and I walk out of the house into the waiting taxi that will take us to the train station.

Relieved to have the awkward moment over with I look forward to the great adventure that awaits me in far-off Canada. The land of snow and ice, as depicted in some of the movies I have seen, starring Jeanette McDonald and Nelson Eddy. Eddy in his Mounties uniform left an indelible image of Canada's frozen north.

Maurice assures me that Canada is not like that. "As a matter of fact, Toronto, where we will be living is very hot and humid in the summer, much hotter than Belgium and much less rain."

We board the train in Kapellenbos and it takes us to Antwerp's Central Station. We have just enough time to offload our luggage and transfer to the train that will take us to Brussels. We manage but with a minute to spare.

"Whew! That was close." Maurice says completely out of breath. He gets an Asthma attack when he is under stress. In Brussels we catch a taxi that will take us to Melsbroek, the International airport. It's much further than we had thought.

The little bit of money that dad gave us, for the months of slave labour, is quickly disappearing. Once in Melsbroek, at the check-in counter, we are assigned our seats and receive boarding passes. It feels like "Deja Vue". I think back to the time that I was on my first plane when dad brought me from Holland to Belgium. We arrived at the same airport, as I recall. The stewardesses are still as pretty and as friendly as I first remember them. They're constantly smiling, reassuring anxious parents and tending to the crying children. A sweet female voice announces, over the intercom, in three languages, French, Flemish and English, that it is now time to board the airplane. Excited because I get the window seat, I settle in for the long flight. Looking at the description card from the seat pocket I notice that the plane is a Douglas DC-7B, a four engine prop plane. It is five pm and the plane starts the ride down to the runway readying for take-off.

Maurice gets airsick and brought along some Gravol.

"I should have taken one before boarding. What should I do now?" he worries out loud.

"Take one now, right away, so it has a chance to start working. You'll be OK."

"Are you sure?"

"For sure" is my unequivocal reply, flattered that he would ask me this very important question.

Without the help of water to wash down the tiny pill he swallows it dry. The pill gets lodged in the back of his throat and now he complains: "You told me it would be OK. The pill is stuck and my throat has gone to sleep. Why did you let me take the pill without water?"

"I thought it would be easy to swallow. Look how tiny the pill is." As I hand him another. "Here take this one too."

"Are you nuts? Haven't you caused me enough trouble?" I attempt to suppress a laugh. It's so funny, but he is not amused. He glares at me. Every so often he levels this accusatory look at me. By now he is paranoid that he will choke on this stupid little pill and he keeps clearing his throat. The stewardess brings a cup of water. Thank goodness, his discomfort becomes less and less as time goes on.

First we fly to Manchester and after landing, the plane is refueled. From my vantage point at the window I get a first hand view of the proceedings.

After about one hour we are cleared for take-off. The meals are served about an hour after leaving Manchester. We have a choice of chicken or beef. Both are quite tasty.

"Maurice isn't surprising that from a small kitchen galley such delicious meals are prepared?

With a hint of triumph in his voice, Maurice tells me, "The meals are prepared on the ground in big flight kitchens and brought on board just before take-off and they are re-heated on the plane."

"I knew that," feeling stupid for not knowing that.

We fly throughout the night to our next destination, Gander Newfoundland. In Gander, with cramped up legs from the very long flight; "Immigration policy prevents us from disembarking," so says the gorgeous stewardess in a sweet voice, "you can, however, move about the plane," she adds with a smile. Who can get mad at that, I think with fire in my loins?

The plane takes flight again and after five hours reaches its final point of debarkation, Montreal. Total flight time including stopovers was a record 24 hours. We are exhausted, dirty and sweaty. This flight was not enjoyable. We gather our luggage and proceed to Immigration.

"Stop right there." someone bellows. This is where I discover the meaning of mindless officialdom. Immigration is a line that we cannot cross until it is our turn to be interviewed by an Immigration officer. Shades of "Orwell's 1984". The interview does not take long and before we know it we are standing outside the arrival lounge at Dorval waiting for the train to take us to our final destination; Toronto's Union station. After a five hour train ride and 29 hours after leaving Belgium, I meet uncle Levie and Auntie Roo, whom I have not seen for more than ten years. They offer us a safe haven, for at least the first little while until we can fend for ourselves or until we have outstayed our welcome. Maurice, who has stayed with them in the past knows them well and engages in easy familiarity. Loekie their eldest son treats Maurice as a brother, though I detect an undertone of derisiveness. Years of distrust into man's true motives have made me a cynic I suppose. My guard goes up. We do, with alacrity, accept their kind offer of a place to hang our hats for a while. I am so tired I think I'll sleep into next week.

CONCLUSION

Anti-Semitism, a word that fills the heart of every Jew with consternation, but elicits only an anemic reaction from the rest of the world. Anti, a Latin word meaning that the person who practices it is against or opposed to something. Webster's dictionary defines anti-Semitism as hostility or hatred towards or prejudice against Jews or Judaism.

The Bible divided mankind into three major races: the Semites, the Hamites and the sons of Japheth. The Semites were the descendants from Shem, son of Noah, Hamites were scions of Ham. The Hamites were black and the Semites were a mixture of black and white, the Japhites had both white and yellow complexions.

The Semites settled in Iraq, Syria and the Arabian Peninsula. "Why the history and geography lesson?" you ask. Simple, to explore the history of Anti-Semitism. Hatred is as old as humanity itself. It dates back to Genesis, as man was pitted against woman and brother against brother, then family against family, then tribe against tribe, then nation against nation. There has never been a shortage of antagonists. But the practice of hatred towards the Jews was promulgated and fine-tuned by the Catholic Church. The Holy See branding the Jews as the killers of Christ and thereby demonizing them for nearly two thousand years.

The practice of Hitler's anti-Semitism in Europe was based on Hitler's classification of people as Aryan and non-Aryan. The non-Aryans, as defined by him, were targeting mostly the Jews, because they were such a huge visible minority in Germany, as well as other races with an Oriental origin. The discrimination was fueled by unfounded fears of a Jewish plot to dominate the German economy and ultimately the entire world and it reached its climax during Hitler's Nazi regime.

The prevailing attitude now, after war's end, is that incidents of local Jewish hatred should be exaggerated to give it the appearance of an organized conspiracy. So this means that anti-Semitism has become politicized. I am of the opinion that anti-Semitism should be fought wherever it rears its ugly head, but not to the extent that it is made to be something that it is not.

To be certain, many countries including America, Canada and Great Britain were quiet on the issue of Hitler's "Final Solution". In all, the evidence of knowledge and inaction is so overwhelming that it has all but destroyed the older liberator image of the Allies in relation to the Holocaust. In the most influential rendering of the new picture, The Abandonment of the Jews: America and the Holocaust, 1941-45, David Wyman, a Christian scholar, gave no quarter:

"America, the land of refuge, offered little succor. American Christians forgot about the Good Samaritan. Even American Jews lacked the unquenchable sense of urgency the crisis demanded. The Nazis were the murderers, but we were the all too passive accomplices...The Holocaust was certainly a Jewish tragedy. But it was not only a Jewish tragedy. It was also a Christian tragedy, a tragedy for Western civilization, and a tragedy for all humankind. The killing was done by people, to other people, while still others stood by."

As a judgment on the American past that developed in a period of general, highly critical reassessment, this vision passed beyond academia into public consciousness and rhetoric. Even before the publication of Wyman's book, the survivor and writer Elie Wiesel spoke for the victims as the evidence of Allied inaction came to the fore.

"During the turmoil the victims were naive enough to feel certain that the so-called civilized world knew nothing of their plight. If the killers could kill freely, it was only because the Allies were not informed. They were wrong. People knew and kept silent. People knew and did nothing. No effort was initiated, no political or military operation undertaken to save them. It was an amazing display of detachment, of laissez faire, demonstrating an attitude shared, in fact, by the leaders of the free Jewish communities."

Such historical judgments have become incorporated into our vision of current affairs.

As early as 1939 as well as during and after the war Canada's prevailing emigration policy for the Jews was; "None is too many"; a reply made by immigration official when a delegation of Jews went to Ottawa in 1939 to ask: "How many Jews will Canada take in?" The Immigration Minister answered, "None is too many". Canada's top bureaucrat in the Immigration Department, Fred Blair wanted no Jews in Canada and did everything he could in the way of roadblocks to prevent it. Mackenzie King's inaction demonstrated that he didn't want to allow Jews into Canada either. Canada certainly had the opportunity to rescue thousands of Jews, but wouldn't budge on its policy of "None is Too Many." That policy continued even after the war when ships laden with the Jews from the concentration camps were denied refuge into Canada. These ships sailed the high seas for more than a year because nobody wanted to provide a safe harbour anywhere. The Jews were all stateless, their citizenship stripped from them by their nations of birth. Mercifully all of them sailed to Palestine where the Zionists smuggled them into the country.

In most cases none but the flimsiest of excuses were given for the refused entry.

I can't help but think that most countries, in quiet acquiescence, applauded Hitler's "Final Solution". If some feel outraged over this remark, then I have to ask,"Did their silence not speak more loudly than words?" The answer most often given as an excuse is: "We did not know."

The disenfranchisement of the German Jews started in full view of the world. The relentless defamation and impoverishment of the Jews went forward with impunity, as early as 1934. They were barred from careers in the civil service, public office, theater and film, broadcasting and journalism. Their properties, businesses, livelihood, their jobs and their privileged positions in society, alongside their German brethren were taken away. They were denied access to hotels, movie houses, restaurants, hospitals, grocery stores and butcher shops. Shop signs proclaimed; "Juden unerwunscht" (Jews not welcome). Jews had all their means to a livelihood taken away. There was no international outrage.

Has history taught us nothing? The question begs to be asked however: Where were the Jews of the United States, Canada and Great Britain when the ships were being turned away? For sure the war has made us paranoid and of a consequence we sadly observe that the years of inaction during the Nazi regime had terrible consequences, the annihilation of six million of us. Was this type of evil-doing too much to contemplate for the world? The white hot anger I still experience towards anything and anyone German must be tempered with the belief and trust in the innate goodness of man, German or not. We're all driven to a summary justice approach when we think that Jews are slighted in any way.

To heal the disease of anti-Semitism today, from a moral, political or educational perspective we must be attuned to its chameleon-like changes. We need to look beyond the conventional niceties of tolerance, diversity or multi-culturalism; even-though these values are practical, pragmatic solutions to an increasingly polarized world.

Nations with a vested, selfish interest must end the despicable international conspiracy to marginalize, demonize, or destroy Israel and its people. The leadership of the United Nations must show some backbone and stand up to the bullying tactics of the Arab nations and their allies, who want nothing better than to push the Israeli people into the sea.

Irshad Manji, best selling author and TV personality asks the question no one dares to ask, "Why was Israel ultimately born and Palestine *stillborn*". What are needed here are some historical facts about Palestine. In 1947, the United nations laid out a plan for the partitioning of the land in question, proposing that forty-five percent of the land would be under Arab rule, while the rest would be set aside for the Jewish state and both entities would share Jerusalem under International supervision. The common complaint from the

Arabs was that the Zionists would have gotten more land. The fact is that the Jewish state would have been largely comprised of the Negev dessert, the least fertile land of the area. The Palestinian state would have had an overwhelming Arab population. The Jewish state would have only had a thin majority of Jews. The Jews reluctantly approved the United Nations plan and six months later declared their independence. The Jews knew they needed a national homeland and correctly traced it back to their earliest and most unrelenting roots; the land the Arabs belatedly called Palestine. Do the Jews have a historical attachment to Palestine? According to a DNA study that was conducted by an international team of researchers and consequently published in the Proceedings of the National Academy of Sciences, Jews and Arabs share at least one ancestor, "with a common Middle Eastern origin," as the study puts it. Islamic tradition concurs, which says that Ishmael, the founder of the Arab nation and Isaac the founder of the Jewish nation were half brothers sired by Abraham. The Prophet Mohammed was a descendant of Ishmael and Moses and Jesus descendants of Isaac. Do Jews have a claim to Palestine?

They do according to the Koran: "We said to the Israelites: "Dwell in the land. When the promise of the hereafter comes to be fulfilled, we shall assemble you all together." The Koran 17:104.

How did Palestinians become refugees within full view of the Arab world?

Within days of Israel's statehood in it's midst, no less than five Arab armies invaded Israel therewith kick starting the Palestinian refugee problem. In some towns Israeli commanders empowered by the Dalet plan, or Plan D. In Hebrew Dalet is the fourth letter, similar to "d" in English. This Plan devised by the Haganah, a Hebrew word meaning "Defense", was a Jewish paramilitary organization in Palestine during the British mandate of Palestine from 1920 to 1948. The Haganah are known to be the foundation of the modern Israel Defense Forces. The purpose of the Plan was, according to its Jewish planners, to defend the establishment of a Jewish state in Palestine. The grief it imposed on Palestinians was undeniable, though in many towns Arabs were urged to remain and thank God many did and accepted Israeli citizenship. Many more Palestinians, however, choose to leave, expecting they would return as soon as the last Israeli had been driven into the sea. Khaled al-Azm, the prime minister of Syria during that period, stated that these refugees took their marching orders not from the Israelis but from their Arab brethren. "In listing the reasons for the Arab failure in 1948, Khaled al-Azm notes that; "Since 1948, it is we who have demanded the return of the refugees, while it is we who made them leave. We brought disaster upon a million Arab refugees by inviting them and bringing pressure on them to leave. We have accustomed them to begging. [W]e have participated in lowering their morale and social level. Then we exploited them in executing crimes of murder, arson and throwing stones upon men, women and children. All this in the service of political purposes."

This collective flight helped the Jews, whose strategic position improved without any work on their part. So much for Israel's one hundred percent culpability for the Palestinian refugee problem.

The United Nations also contributes to the problem by declaring 3.5 million Palestinians to be refugees. Original refugees numbered 700,000, but the U.N. also defines their children and grandchildren as refugees. Sadly one third of them still live in urban camps surrounded by gleaming high rises and private Palestinian villas. This is totally unnecessary. After all, hundreds of thousands of Jews found themselves evicted from Arab lands, yet they didn't languish in refugee camps because Israel took them all in, with open arms. As a matter of record Israel also granted citizenship to one hundred thousand Palestinians under a family reunification plan. What have Arab nations done in contrast? They let them languish in camps or worse.

After the 1991 Persian Gulf War, Kuwait kicked out at least three hundred thousand Palestinians from inside its borders as payback for Yasser Arafat's support of Saddam Hussein. "Most of the evicted Palestinians never knew Palestine or any other country, except Kuwait," notes Kanan Makiya, author of a book on cruelty and silence in the Arab world. "Besides kicking them out," he says, "semi official vigilante groups arbitrarily arrested other Palestinians and made them disappear or gunned them down or tortured them in public and killed them."

Talk about Arab hypocrisy. For years Kuwait donated much less than Israel to the United Nations agency that cares for Palestinian refugees. As far as Saudi Arabia with its bulging money vaults, the Saudis refuse to take in Palestinians refugees and make them Saudi citizens. They will however raise millions for the financing of suicide bombers. Lebanon cares even less, its laws prohibiting most Palestinian refugees from working full-time, purchasing land, or becoming professionals. They simply have to get by on odd jobs. The only Arab nation that has extended citizenship to Palestinian refugees is Jordan and that is because most Jordanians are Palestinian anyway.

Now back to History 101. In the early 20th Century we are led to believe that Zionists came into Palestine and started turfing out Palestinians. That is untrue. The instruction to the Palestinians to vacate did not start with the Jews. The Ottoman Empire, Turkish Muslims, oversaw Palestine, and against the better interest of the Arab tenant farmers, voluntarily sold off land to the early Zionists. And they did so with impunity, despite cabled protests from one hundred and fifty high profile Arabs. Protests that were ignored by the Ottomans.

During the First World War, the Arabs helped Britain fight the Ottomans with the promise that all of Palestine would be in Arab hands afterwards. This deal was brokered through the British high commissioner for Egypt and the Sudan, Sir Henry McMahon, in a series of private letters in 1915. In 1917, the Balfour Declaration broke the presumed pact with the Arabs, by committing some of Palestine to the Jews. The Brits bested the Bible by making the "Promised Land" the "twice-promised land". The Arabs felt betrayed and they were. But so were the Jews. In the year 1921, the land that was promised to the Jews for a Jewish homeland, almost four fifth of that went to the Arabs for what would eventually become Jordan.

A mere two years later Britain gave more Jewish territory away, this time to Syria.

Here is a name that lives on in infamy, enter the Mufti of Jerusalem, Haj Amin el-Husseini, he became the duly elected president of the Supreme Muslim Council in 1922. Though he was elected, he stubbornly clung to power for fifteen years. His single-minded intent was to rid Palestine of all Jews and in doing so was not above authorizing the serial murder of Arabs that got in the way. As the Nazi menace swelled in Europe so did Jewish migration to the Middle East. Those who showed the least bit of sympathy to the Jews could expect a visit from a body of Haj Amin's gunmen. A number of Arabs asked the British for protection. Haj Amin blamed the Jews for the inner terror that his men created. In 1939, Britain having had their fill of trouble in the Middle East and anxious to focus on defeating Hitler offered the Palestinians a plan for full statehood. It was proposed that Arabs and Jews would inhabit a single territory, to come under Palestinian control in ten years. At the same time, Jewish land purchases would be drastically curtailed. And after independence, the Palestinians could devise their own immigration policies. That's autonomy in anybody's book. "Not good enough," wails the Mufti of Jerusalem, whom the British wouldn't talk to directly. "We want independence in five years; otherwise you can shove the deal." But Haj never consulted the poor sods that worked the land; they were the ones that got shafted in the end. According to a British newspaper article in 1938 most villagers "have no great sympathy with the Arab rebels that are trying to stem the flood of Jewish immigrants and are clambering for an Arab government for Palestine. Impoverished by their own Chiefs and finding themselves economically deprived, eight former Palestinian commandos charged the Mufti with misusing millions of pounds, without being able to point at the building of a single mosque or school or a hospital. Did he even build an asylum or a cistern from which the poor could drink? During the Nazi years, good old boy Haj Amin, the same guy that practiced his assassination skills on his fellow Arabs, pressured the British to turn away boatloads of Jewish refugees. Some drowned in the Mediterranean; some were returned to the gas chambers and crematoriums of Europe. The Mufti did not stop there, stopping Croatian children, many of them orphaned, from entering the Holy Land. He figured that merely stemming the Jewish population growth would not be enough to guarantee an Arab Palestine. For this he made the decision to align himself on the winning side of the war by betting on Hitler. Haj Amin paid the Fuhrer a personal visit and the Mufti's blond hair and blue eyes became convincing barometers of credibility, comforting Hitler that, in his own words, Haj Amin "may well be descended from Roman stock." Many other Muslims hitched their futures on a Nazi victory and Haj Amin broadcast Nazi propaganda in the Arab world. "Kill the Jews wherever you find them. This pleases God, history and religion. This saves your honour. God is with you."

Although he lost his gamble on Hitler, he escaped being branded as a war criminal. Arrested in France he smuggled himself out of Allied detention and eventually wound up in Egypt.

An engineer named Arafat, whose real name is el-Husseini, and that makes him a member of Haj Amin's clan will be eager to learn the ropes of leadership from his nemesis. He learned well. He picked up tips for rejecting peace with Israel, waging terror on his own people, and wasting millions intended for development. Instead of accepting a perfectly good United Nations plan in 1947 and co-exist with the Jewish state, they rejected it and by waging war they managed to lose even more land. Ironic isn't?

In 1948 the Arabs thought they had found their new Saladin in Egypt's Gamal Abdul Nasser, who with Stalin's help would defeat Israel. The Egyptian self appointed General turned President became a hero to the Arab world by thumbing his nose at the United States, Israel's most enthusiastic cheerleader. Nasser OD'd on Stalin's new ideological opiate and equated anti-Americanism with anti-colonianism, staking his future and that of his people on cultural renaissance and secularism. Nasser and his Arab buddies grew mesmerized by the dream of avenging the Zionist occupation, and secular socialism became its rallying banner. And instead of victory they met with further dishonour. Israel bested Egypt and its allies in the 1967 war, with the resulting, inconceivable loss of Jerusalem. It caused the emasculation of the once mighty Arab nation's identity and the death of the new Socialism. Religious fundamentalists were eager to jump into the breach with bumper-sticker assurances that "Islam is the solution."

"Their great hope has been that a return to strict Islam would provide the strength for a final victory over Zionism and Israel" So says Egyptian liberal Gaber Asfour.

From shiny new secularism to mind-numbing Islam fundamentalism in one generation has brought us full circle in the Middle East. Strict Islam is gaining momentum and Yasser Arafat managed to adapt religious vocabulary for his own political agenda. The word "martyr" for instance has been borrowed from the Koran, without the religious connotation, and invoked to signify something much less than its heroic Koranic meaning. Arafat's use of Islam as a spiritual machete has been no solution at all. Even in some Muslim quarters there are rumblings of mistrust for the current tactics. "Everything seemed doomed to failure and corruption," says Arab Israeli professor Muhammad Abu Samra. Its sentiment is a street-level summary in Palestine. A former minister in Arafat's cabinet, Nabil Amr, wrote an appeal for introspection in one of the Palestinian Authority's official newspaper, thereby risking his security.

"We take comfort, Mr. President, in designing excuses." He accused Arafat of squandering the world's aid and goodwill, as well as a legitimate offer for a peaceful co-existence with Israel. He exposed the tribal mindset of Palestinian politicians while they were masquerading as emancipated democrats. In closing he wrote,"We committed serious mistakes against our people, our Authority, and our dream of statehood. To make up for these mistakes, we must confess our failure first, and then take immediate action. Our people are noble and deserve from us the commitment to think with them and for their benefit. We cannot let our people's destiny be set free to chance, a chance that, under a new world order, may take yet another eternal struggle without opening a door of hope."

Nabil Amr survived the bullets shot at his house. As a positive result of his rhetoric, more Palestinians are echoing his sentiments in public. They've acknowledged that Israel is not the primary source of their oppression. So why is it that so many in the West still perceive Israel as the cold blooded, ruthless aggressor and purveyor of death and destruction?

It is quite evident to the leaders of Israel that "an eye for an eye" policy is an effective way to combat terrorism and that a policy of non-violence in the face of extreme provocation elicits only contempt on the part of the terrorists. Israel will continue to demonstrate its resolve to do what is necessary to maintain its security and independent nationhood. We have no other choice. Jews worldwide have a close kinship with Israel. It was foretold in the Bible. The world needs Israel. Nothing less will suffice.

What then can we do, as individuals, to combat anti-Semitism, racism and other forms of discrimination? Meet force with force? Turn the other cheek? I don't know. We can, however, demonstrate to the world that we as members of the human family do not tolerate racism of any kind. Too often we Jews bemoan the fact that we are being discriminated against while at the same time we discriminate against others, whether it is directed at Christians, Moslems or other groups. We all do it, not always with malignant intent. It is ingrained in our everyday language. Words that describe a race or a colour of people can be, at the same time, a racial put-down. Traditions and words that are permissible to be used today may no longer be politically correct tomorrow.

To laugh at ourselves is a form of therapy, but to laugh at others is not funny. Jewish jokes told by non-Jews are not very funny and often offensive, as well as ethnic jokes told by Jews about other groups are equally offensive. If we show forth a scrupulous adherence to non-discrimination, even in the face of extreme provocation, it might demonstrate to the world that we are serious and unequivocal in our non-racist approach to all.

We must lobby for equal rights for all and when we experience personal racism we must stand firm in pointing out that we will not tolerate it. We must do this, preferably, in a non-violent manner.

Will this work? I wonder, but it is worth a try. We know from the Nazi holocaust that doing nothing in the face of total annihilation is not the answer. Armed conflict could have worked. But if everyone in the world would have raised the banner for the Jewish plight, as the brave people in Denmark did when they demonstrated civil disobedience, by all wearing a Star of David, then we might have been spared the great loss in human life and despair that was endured at the hands of the Nazis. The Nazis could only do what they did because of the inaction and silence of the rest of the world. That empowered Hitler to become bolder and bolder as he realized that no matter what excesses he perpetrated on the Jews of Europe, no nation would speak out in defense of the Jews. The collective will to stop him could have stopped him.

But, you see, it suited the nations of the world to do nothing. Let Hitler do their dirty work and after, bemoan the fact that this happened. This is part of the disease of anti-Semitism, it is rooted in the mistaken belief that Jews are too strong, too powerful, too rich, too controlling of the world's finances and commerce and must be stopped.

In retrospect, doing nothing, allowed 12 million people, 6 million Jews and 6 million non-Jews, to perish in Hitler's concentration camps.

In everything I seek, is justice. That is my motivating principle based on experiences from my early life that was bereft of human contingencies.

Great evil was perpetrated on my brother and me. So great that much of my story defies telling. Mere words are not able to encompass this monstrous evil. This kind of evil is the absence of God. It is nothingness. Nothingness has no words.

And then, by chance I discovered a prayer of the Baha'i Faith. At first the meaning escapes me, but then, after careful contemplation, it provides the backdrop for a deeper understanding of the human condition and the frailty of man. It dawns on me that, as a society, the choices we make are collective choices, and the mistakes we make are collective mistakes, and the transgressions are collective transgressions, and the sins are collective sins, but inaction is my sin. We, each of us, as members of the human race, have the responsibility to act for the common good, whatever that encompasses. Let's not merely be spectators in a world that demands answers but full, active and equal participants. Take issues out of the realm of the mundane into the mondiale. What is needed in this complex existence we call life are more bold, passionate and world embracing ideas. Ideas are what set us apart from the rest of the animal world. Let your conscience be your guide. Get involved. We all matter. There is a reckoning. There is a God.

EPILOGUE

FIRE TABLET

In the Name of God, the Most Ancient, the Most Great.

Indeed the hearts of the sincere are consumed in the fire of separation: Where is the gleaming of the light of Thy Countenance, O Beloved of the worlds?

Those who are near unto Thee have been abandoned in the darkness of desolation: Where is the shining of the morn of Thy reunion, O Desire of the worlds?

The bodies of Thy chosen ones lie quivering on distant sands: Where is the ocean of Thy presence, O Enchanter of the worlds?

Longing hands are uplifted to the heaven of Thy grace and generosity: Where are the rains of Thy bestowal, O Answerer of the worlds?

The infidels have arisen in tyranny on every hand: Where is the compelling power of Thine ordaining pen, O Conqueror of the worlds?

The barking of dogs is loud on every side: Where is the lion of the forest of Thy might, O Chastiser of the worlds?

Coldness hath gripped all mankind: Where is the warmth of Thy love, O Fire of the worlds?

Calamity hath reached its height: Where are the signs of Thy succor, O Salvation of the worlds?

Darkness hath enveloped most of the peoples: Where is the brightness of Thy splendor, O Radiance of the worlds?

The necks of men are stretched out in malice: Where are the swords of Thy vengeance, O Destroyer of the worlds?

Abasement hath reached its lowest depth: Where are the emblems of Thy glory, O Glory of the worlds?

Sorrows have afflicted the Revealer of Thy Name, the All Merciful: Where is the joy of the Dayspring of Thy Revelation, O Delight of the worlds?

Anguish hath befallen all the peoples of the earth: Where are the ensigns of Thy gladness, O Joy of the worlds?

Thou seest the Dawning Place of Thy signs veiled by evil suggestions: Where are the fingers of Thy might, O Power of the worlds?

Sore thirst hath overcome all men: Where is the river of Thy bounty, O Mercy of the worlds?

Greed hath made captive all mankind: Where are the embodiments of detachment, O Lord of the worlds?

Thou seest this Wronged One lonely in exile: Where are the hosts of the heaven of Thy Command, O Sovereign of the worlds?

I have been forsaken in a foreign land: Where are the emblems of Thy faithfulness, O Trust of the worlds?

The agonies of death have laid hold on all men: Where is the surging of Thine Ocean of eternal life, O Life of the worlds?

The whisperings of Satan have been breathed to every creature: Where is the meteor of Thy fire, O Light of the worlds?

The drunkenness of passion hath perverted most of mankind: Where are the daysprings of purity, O Desire of the worlds?

Thou seest this Wronged One veiled in tyranny among the Syrians: Where is the radiance of Thy dawning light, O Light of the worlds?

Thou seest Me forbidden to speak forth: Then from where will spring Thy melodies, O Nightingale of the worlds?

Most of the people are enwrapped in fancy and idle imaginings: Where are the exponents of Thy certitude, O Assurance of the worlds?

Bahá is drowning in a sea of tribulation: Where is the Ark of Thy salvation, O Savior of the worlds?

Thou seest the Dayspring of Thine utterance in the darkness of creation: Where is the sun of the heaven of Thy grace, O Lightgiver of the worlds?

The lamps of truth and purity, of loyalty and honor, have been put out: Where are the signs of Thine avenging wrath, O Mover of the worlds?

Canst Thou see any who have championed Thy Self, or who ponder on what hath befallen Him in the pathway of Thy love? Now doth My pen halt, O Beloved of the worlds?

The branches of the Divine Lote-Tree lie broken by the onrushing gales of destiny: Where are the banners of Thy succor, O Champion of the worlds?

This Face is hidden in the dust of slander: Where are the breezes of Thy compassion, O Mercy of the worlds?

The robe of sanctity is sullied by the people of deceit: Where is the vesture of Thy holiness, O Adorner of the worlds?

The sea of grace is stilled for what the hands of men have wrought: Where are the waves of Thy bounty, O Desire of the worlds?

The door leading to the Divine Presence is locked through the tyranny of Thy foes: Where is the key of Thy bestowal, O Unlocker of the worlds?

The leaves are yellowed by the poisoning winds of sedition: Where is the downpour of the clouds of Thy bounty, O Giver of the worlds?

The universe is darkened with the dust of sin: Where are the breezes of Thy forgiveness, O Forgiver of the worlds?

This Youth is lonely in a desolate land: Where is the rain of Thy heavenly grace, O Bestower of the worlds?

O Supreme Pen, We have heard Thy most sweet call in the eternal realm: Give Thou ear unto what the Tongue of Grandeur uttereth, O Wronged One of the worlds?

Were it not for the cold, how would the heat of Thy words prevail, O Expounder of the worlds?

Were it not for calamity, how would the sun of Thy patience shine, O Light of the worlds?

Lament not because of the wicked. Thou wert created to bear and endure, O Patience of the worlds.

How sweet was Thy dawning on the horizon of the Covenant among the stirrers of sedition, and Thy yearning after God, O Love of the worlds.

By Thee the banner of independence was planted on the highest peaks, and the sea of bounty surged, O Rapture of the worlds.

By Thine aloneness the Sun of Oneness shone, and by Thy banishment the land of Unity was adorned. Be patient, O Thou Exile of the worlds.

We have made abasement the garment of glory, and affliction the adornment of Thy temple, O Pride of the worlds.

Thou seest the hearts are filled with hate, and to overlook is Thine, O Thou Concealer of the sins of the worlds.

When the swords flash, go forward! When the shafts fly, press onward! O Thou Sacrifice of the worlds.

Dost Thou wail, or shall I wail? Rather shall I weep at the fewness of Thy champions, O Thou Who hast caused the wailing of the worlds.

Verily, I have heard Thy call, O All-Glorious Beloved; and now is the face of Bahá flaming with the heat of tribulation and with the fire of Thy shining word, and He hath risen up in faithfulness at the place of sacrifice, looking toward Thy pleasure, O Ordainer of the worlds.

O Ali-Akbar, thank thy Lord for this Tablet whence thou canst breathe the fragrances of My meekness, and know what hath beset Us in the path of God, the Adored of all the worlds.

Should all the servants read and ponder this, there shall be kindled in their veins a fire that shall set aflame the worlds.

- Bahá'u'lláh

BIBLIOGRAPHY:

Ashkenazi Jews in Amsterdam; *Edward van Voolen*: Communities Main Page www.bh.org.il/communities/index/aspx

War Statistics in the Netherlands WWII http://members.iinet.net.au/~gduncan/1944.html#lesser_known_1944

Theodor Hertzl Der Judenstaat, , http://www.wzo.org.il/home/movement/herzl1.htm

Asfour Gaber, quoted in, *New Perspectives Quarterly*, Winter 2002. "Osama bin Laden: Financier of Intolerant 'Desert' Islam." Download at www.digitalnpq.org

Proceedings of the National Academy of Sciences of the United States of America, Volume 97, Issue 12, June 6, 2000, p. 10

Arendt Hannah:All sorrows can be borne if they are put into a story: The Human Condition by Hannah Arendt (University of Chicago Press, (This quote is presented as the inspirational heading to a chapter titled "Action." No source is given.)

Abells Irving, Troper Harold: None Is Too Many: Canada and the Jews of Europe 1933-1948, Lester Pub Ltd; 3rd edition (June 1997) (Paperback)

Bahá'u'lláh, Fire Tablet: (Compilations, Baha'i Prayers, p. 214), Baha'i Publishing Trust, Wilmette IL. 60091

Berenbaum, Michael. "The World Must Know: The History Of

The Holocaust As Told In The United States Holocaust Memorial Museum." New York: Little, Brown and Company, 1993.

Breitman, Richard. "Official Secrets: What the Nazis Planned, What the British and Americans Knew." New York: Hill & Wang, 1999.

Chesnoff Richard, Pack of Thieves, Doubleday Publishing, a division of Random House Inc. New York.

Frank Anne, Anne Frank Diary of a Young Girl, Knopf Publishing, 1994

A Plea for the Survivors: published originally in the New York Times Magazine, August 1978)

Michman Joseph, Hartog Beem Pinkas: Geschiedenis Van De Joodse Gemeenschap in Netherland (Joseph Michman, "the Jewish community in Holland"), Jerusalem: Yad Vashem, 1999, Yad Vashem Studies on the European Jewish Catastrophe and Resistance by Livia Rothkirchen
Review author[s]: Lucy S. Dawidowicz
American Historical Review, Vol. 81, No. 3 (Jun. 1976) pp. 579-580

Dr. J. Presser: Ondergang: De Vervolging en Verdelging van het Nederlandse Jodendom 1940-1945; Part I and II (The Persecution and Destruction of the Dutch Jews): Published by The Hague State Publisher 1965, Authorized by the Secretary of Education, Arts and Science. This book is represented by monograph number 10 Institute War documentation.

Wyman David S, The Abandonment Of The Jews: America and the Holocaust, New York: Pantheon Books,

Meir-Levi David, Arabs Fled from Palestine in 1948: SOURCE BIG LIES: Demolishing The Myths of the Propaganda War Against Israel,

Makiya, Kanan, Cruelty and Silence: War, Tyranny, Uprising and the Arab World (W. W. Norton and Company 500 Fifth Ave. New York, NY 1994)

D.N.
MSY

Made in the USA
Charleston, SC
21 July 2016